A Star in his
own Imagination

A Star in his own Imagination

Published by The Conrad Press in the United Kingdom 2020

Tel: +44(0)1227 472 874
www.theconradpress.com
info@theconradpress.com

ISBN 978-1-913567-11-8

Typesetting and Cover Design by:
Charlotte Mouncey, www.bookstyle.co.uk

The Conrad Press logo was designed by Maria Priestley.

Printed and bound in Great Britain by Clays Ltd, Elcograf S.p.A.

A Star in his
own Imagination

Paul Allen

Chapter 1

Struck down in my prime

Once there was a man, an ordinary man who wanted nothing more than for each day to follow another and to enjoy his life and the love of his wonderful wife.

But then something happened momentous enough to turn his world completely upside down and change his life for ever, something profound enough to force him to question his very existence.

What happened was that on Tuesday the third of July 2012, he had a massive stroke.

That man was me.

I woke up in the early hours of the morning.

I had a headache on my left side and was tingling on my right. I dozed for an hour or so, then everything was reversed. The headache had moved from the left to the right side and the tingling was all down my body on the left. My wife Liz was even more upset than I was, so she phoned for an ambulance.

The paramedics were not sure it was a stroke. They could only offer me a bed in one of the two hospitals they served, neither of which had a good reputation. I reluctantly chose one and soon we arrived. I don't remember the next few hours, but I woke up strapped naked to some sort of scanner.

Two young men in an inner office chatted to each other until one realised it was going home time. They put on their coats turned off the lights and left. Two nurses realised my plight and released me from my captivity, equipped me with a gown to hide my modesty and got me to bed.

I woke up days later in ICU.

It was then I was told I had suffered an enormous stroke and had stopped breathing. The A&E crash team resuscitated me and put me on a ventilator to assist my breathing. They also put me in a medically induced coma while they decided what to do next.

It didn't take me long to realise I couldn't speak, me whose favourite saying is, 'why use one word when fifteen will do', it was like nature's little joke. I was kept for seven weeks in the Intensive Care Unit (ICU).

Here I learnt two things, first, what I had suffered had a name, 'Locked-In Syndrome', which leaves you with none of your body function except the brain. Not a very good start in my case, secondly the hospital was ill equipped to offer any rehabilitation, only recuperation. For this you would have to look for a private hospital, immediately my lovely wife Liz searched for another hospital.

This time she came up trumps and found The Raphael Medical centre in Hildenborough, near Tonbridge, Kent. So, a few days later and seven weeks after my stroke, we were welcomed by a member of staff who we now know is Sister Mary. I was placed in Tobias House, which is a high-dependency unit.

Later, I wrote this about Tobias House:

This is a great hospital with superb staff. The carers balance looking after an individual with excellent interpersonal skills and humour.

Similarly, the nurses have all the skills necessary to look after patients but with a wonderful bedside manner and sense of humour. The therapists and doctors are all technically excellent, balanced with a charming friendly manner and that obligatory sense of humour. I count a few of these as my friends. I'd like to think they feel the same about me, but I could be kidding myself.

The staff here are truly cosmopolitan, I can say thank you, in twenty-seven different languages. Of course, the other words are a bit more difficult. The gardens are impressive and extensive, natural but with a well-kept manicured appearance. Wait! What am I saying, I am stuck in a wheelchair, paralysed from the neck down, unable to speak with no ability to swallow and only partial sight and hearing I think I will change my name to 'LUCKY.'

The only problem with this place is that it's twenty-five miles from home. I thought nobody would visit me. How wrong could I be? My lovely wife has made a list of visitors to date, there has been 120 friends and relatives come to visit and dozens of messages from well-wishers. Three friends have even performed two concerts for us here. I didn't know I had such friends, or so many. Apparently, I am on the prayer list of fifteen churches and two friends have organised services in my name. They must be confusing me with somebody else.

One of the occupational therapists here has designed me a communication system which effectively divides the alphabet into three sets. By blinking one eye I can indicate the appropriate set. A further blink indicates the exact letter. Of course, this is a very slow process but with experience words can be guessed, speeding up enormously. Liz holds the record for this. She once constructed a whole sentence with only 2 characters. I knew I was getting better when I first tried the system on Liz; she said all I needed for *a complete recovery was a strong will. Without hesitation I asked 'who is Will'*

Sometimes when I am feeling sorry for myself, I ask, 'why me'?

I am reminded of my blessings, I am very happily married, and we own a large six- bedroomed house which Liz is currently downsizing to a three bedroomed bungalow for better wheelchair access. We each drive a Mercedes so the answer to my first question, 'why me?' is a most emphatic 'why not?'

I am glad I had the stroke. It has shown me how many friends I have and the length to which some will go for me.

It has made me examine my lifestyle. Many of my friends have too. It has shown me how hard all the wonderful people here all work. I am sure some of them want me to recover almost as much as I do. It has made me realise how much I have taken for granted. It has reminded me how much I love my darling wife. There are many uncertainties in life but of one thing I am sure. If my wife had not made the phone call and the crash team had not resuscitated me, I would not be here to write this book. So, God bless you all, and I hope this never happens to you.

Chapter 2

Beginnings

To start my story, I must go back to when I was a baby. I was born in Croydon Maternity hospital on Friday 13 January 1956.

When I was about two, one of the neighbours, a Mrs Grimble, saw me in my pushchair and said what an adorable little boy. I had only been speaking a short while and I looked adoringly into her eyes and said,

'I hate you, Grimble.'

Now I may not have known what I was saying, but she obviously did, because I never saw her again.

I was brought up in a council prefab with no central heating. In the winter I was bathed in an enamel bath in front of the fire. I guess I was about four when I used a tennis racket as a guitar and entertained my relatives with Lonnie Donegan songs.

In the spring of that year, Croydon Council moved us to a house in Elmers End. One warm summer's day a neighbour was kind enough to take me to the open-air swimming pool at Purley Way. I saw all the other kids running and jumping in, so I thought I would join them.

Unfortunately, I slipped and banged my head on the way in. I sat on the bottom, unconscious and breathing in water. Apparently, the lifeguard was very quick to act. He dived in and pulled me up out of the water. He then pumped the water out of my lungs and got me breathing again. In that moment I knew why they were called lifeguards. He had literally saved my life. However, I was traumatised by the experience and to this day I still can't put my head under water.

Each week a lorry came to our road selling fruit, vegetables and sweets. You had to step up into the lorry to make your selection. One day, my friends dared each other to steal some sweets and coerced me into joining them. I took the cheapest thing I could find which was a penny liquorice, that is one old penny, not one pence. I felt so ashamed that afterwards I couldn't eat the liquorice and so I gave it away.

As the 5 November approached, Dad invited his friends, Joan and Doug, with their son, Bernard to spend Guy Fawkes Night with us. Dad was sure that Doug would bring a big box of fireworks because he was fairly rich, and he owned a chain of newsagents. Dad was determined not to be outdone however, so amongst *his* fireworks was a very big and impressive looking rocket. Bernard was the same age as me and was one of my best friends.

We had a wonderful firework display and Dad left his rocket as the grand finale. Unfortunately, he used a milk bottle to launch it. At the last moment, the milk bottle fell over, the rocket shot along the grass, through the fence and set fire to next door's runner beans. 'Old Beans' next door came shuffling down his garden looking perplexed. He watched in disbelief as his pride and joy went up in flames. My dad was mortified but Bernard and I thought it was a wonderful conclusion to the fireworks display.

At the age of five I started Monks Orchard Infant School and

I had fallen in love for the first time, with Theresa. We used to walk hand in hand and promised that we would marry when we were older. Sadly, two things happened, we moved again to South Norwood, and I changed schools. Within a month I had forgotten all about Theresa. Love is so fickle when you are five.

After we had moved, I started sleeping with my trusty torch every Christmas eve. I would usually wake in the early hours of Christmas morning and raid my sack of presents. I would then take each present and my torch under the covers to unwrap them. Trying very hard not to disturb my elder brother, Dave, who I shared a room with. Once I had seen the presents I would re-wrap them, most unconvincingly. Hours later I would open them again, this time in front of my parents, feigning surprise.

I must have been eight or nine when I began doubting the existence of Father Christmas. That Christmas Eve, I slept with my torch as per usual but also scheming to surprise whoever was delivering my presents. I managed to wake up not long after I heard someone entering my room and starting to fill my sack. I was about to sit up and turn on my torch, when I had a last minute thought. If it were Father Christmas, he would be angry and may take my presents. If it were Dad, as I suspected, he would give me a slap and then take my presents back. Either way, I decided that discretion was the better part of valour and kept my eyes tightly shut. To this day I am not sure whether or not Father Christmas exists!

Chapter 3

Remember the days of the old school yard
(Cat Stevens)

Overall, my education was good, but one school stands out above all others in my mind. I don't remember much about Monks Orchard infant school, except Theresa, nor about Cyprus infant school. I then crossed the road and went to Cypress Junior School. My memories of that school are somewhat sporadic. I remember it being a good school but not much else.

Bob Benn, one of my friends, was a very fast runner. He won all the running events at sports day. He went on to join Croydon Harriers and ran with some famous athletes, including Seb Coe, helping them to improve their times.

In my last year at Cypress Junior school, I failed my eleven plus by two percent. This meant that I couldn't follow in my brother and sister's footsteps and go to the school of my choice, which was Selhurst Grammar School.

Instead, I found myself in the academic stream of Ashburton Secondary Modern School for Boys. In fact, it was pretty much the best thing that could have ever happened to me. Ashburton was a great school, led by George Manning who was such a good headmaster, he was awarded an OBE.

I admit that I had a rocky start as I was hopeless at sport and was one of the last to be picked for a football or cricket team. Our PE master had no time for any boy who was no good at sport. I was put on the map when I was cast as Oliver in the school production of the show with the same name.

From the third year onwards, Mrs Richards taught us History. During our fourth year the timetables for history and geography clashed, so we were forced to choose which O-Level we wished to take. I didn't much like the geography teacher so, faced with the choice between him and Mrs Richards, I chose history.

My favourite teacher without a doubt was Don Mann. He taught me history in my formative years and French to O-Level. He was the co-producer of the school production of *Oliver*, and he played the part of Fagin. He was great fun to work with, give or take the odd toasting fork up my nose. We had another teacher who taught us French in the first two years, but with a Northern accent. Mr. Mann's accent was far better, and he often worked with us and a French assistant. All I know is that I attained an A grade at O-Level. Either, I had an aptitude for language, or Mr. Mann was an excellent teacher. I think it might have been both.

This was a time before corporal punishment was abolished in schools and some of our masters could be a bit brutal at times. One master used to slipper naughty boys, only he used a size twelve plimsoll. One day, my Chinese friend, Moon Wyecheung, was very naughty and was hauled in front of the class by the teacher. The teacher bent him over and reached for his plimsoll. He hit Cheung as hard as he could, but Cheung didn't cry. Frustrated by his failure to make him cry, the teacher took a run-up from the door, leaping in the air at the last minute. He hit Cheung so hard that he flew across the classroom, but still didn't cry. Cheung told me, the next day, that he had eaten with his family that night and had excused himself early to do his homework. He then cried all night. He had kept back the tears all that time. I have never known such bravery.

One teacher had a deadly aim with a blackboard rubber. If a boy committed a minor misdemeanour, the teacher would hurl the rubber at him. If he committed a more serious offence the teacher would grab him by the sideburns and pull him upwards. The victim would then scramble onto his chair, or even his desk, to try to outreach him. It didn't often work as the teacher was very tall. One boy annoyed the teacher so much that he slammed the palm of his hand on his desk, splitting the lid.

I was never naughty, and I kept my nose buried in my books. I was labelled a swot. I wasn't, it was just self- preservation.

I'm afraid I have given here a pretty dim view of my school, but it wasn't all that bad. There were a couple of rough teachers but, overall, I thoroughly enjoyed my time there.

I was born on Friday the thirteenth so, contrary to the rest of the world, it was always very lucky for me. We once had a maths exam on Friday the thirteenth. I found it so easy and, for the first time in my life, I finished early. I got a hundred percent and the lowest mark was seven percent. I was accused of cheating, but I have never cheated in my life, and anyway, who would I copy from? The boy who came second got eighty percent.

When I was thirteen the school built an outdoor swimming pool. I loved the water, but I couldn't put my head under because I still suffered from post-traumatic effects which I experienced nine years previously. One day the PE teacher ordered us to put our heads under the water, so I tried to explain that

I couldn't, but that wasn't good enough. He leapt into the pool and dunked me. I panicked, gasped and filled my lungs up with water. I had to be dragged out of the pool, the water pumped out of me, and an ambulance called. If I ever had any 'street cred', it was all gone now.

This was not helped when, a year later, I was sitting on the grass with my friend Bill, enjoying the summer sun on a fine day, when suddenly Peter, another classmate who I thought was a friend, kicked me in the head. He was ordered to do so by Byrd, our local teenage gangster, as part of his initiation into the gang. Byrd had been expelled years before and had started his own gang, coming onto the playground, only if there were no teachers around. The force of the blow knocked me over, but I was so incensed that I refused to cry or show any emotion whatsoever. I never spoke to Peter again.

After we finished our O-Levels, we were still expected to come to school even though we had nothing to do. Fortunately, we weren't expected to wear uniform. One Friday lunchtime, a small group of us sneaked out of school and went to a pub in Croydon. To our horror, we spotted one of the more violent teachers sitting at the bar. What was worse was that he saw us. As he came over, we sat trembling in our seats, but thankfully he was very pleasant and bought us all a drink. We chatted and he explained why he instilled fear in first and second year boys; there was no need for discipline after that. Thinking about it, he was right.

Also, in my last year, I was introduced to Chris Rogers, who lived in a flat opposite the school. He was a prominent hi-fi reviewer and speaker designer. He was often asked by manufacturers to give their equipment a good review in return for keeping the product. Chris, would never do that, he would always give an honest and accurate evaluation. He once told a manufacturer, 'if your product is worthy of a bad review, why would I want it?'

I spent many a happy evening in his flat, listening to records through the latest hi-fi.

I left the school the same year that George Manning retired from being headmaster. Loss of one of us made the school decline rapidly, but I think it was George! He was replaced by a person who tried to change everything. There is a saying which is very appropriate for this situation, 'if it ain't broke, don't fix it'. Most of the teachers couldn't work under the new regime, and consequently, half of them resigned.

The new headmaster, unsurprisingly, jumped ship and Don Mann took over as acting headmaster. It was too late to save the school as the damage had been done. When Don retired, the school was closed, and the building was bulldozed. In its place, they built a new adult learning village. It was very sad indeed.

After Ashburton Secondary, I went to Selhurst Grammar School, to study for A levels. I took pure maths, applied maths and physics. My timing couldn't have been worse; it was the year that Selhurst Grammar became a comprehensive. The kids from the rougher schools regarded me as a snob, whilst The Croydonians , boys from Selhurst Grammar, thought I was inferior.

'I say, you comprehensive tyke, how many O-Levels did you get?' One Croydonian asked me.

To this, I answered honestly, that I had eight.

'Oh,' well done, that's not bad for a comprehensive tyke. Of course, I got twelve,' he added.

'I say, grammar school tyke, how many O-Levels did you take?' I replied, summoning the best posh voice I could muster and playing a hunch.

'I took thirteen, if it is any of your business.'

'Oh, bad luck 'old bean', you failed one. I didn't fail any. We could only take eight.'

This is only one example of the torment I faced during my time at Selhurst School. One boy threatened to beat me up after school. I wouldn't have minded if he was on his own, but I was sure that his gang would be with him. It wasn't a good atmosphere for me to learn in so, after I had passed my first- year exams, I left. Soon after I left the school, I joined the Greater London Council as a trainee civil engineer, and they sponsored me to do an Ordinary National Certificate (ONC) at Brixton School of Building.

After I had got my ONC in civil engineering I went next door to the Polytechnic of the South Bank, now called the Southbank University, to do a Higher National Certificate (HNC). It involved one long day and two evening classes at the college.

In the middle of one evening class, I was caught telling my friends a rude joke, which had a very graphic end, and involved me standing up and making gestures. The lecturer saw me and asked me if I wished to share the joke with the class. Naturally, I declined saying that it wasn't a very funny joke. This was a lie, the joke was hilarious, but also very rude. When I passed my HNC I joined the Metropolitan Police service as a trainee programmer. Over the next few years, I took various courses, from programming, systems analysis and project management, to time management, staff management and general management. With all that education and training under my belt, naturally, I became a wedding photographer!

Chapter 4

If music be the food of love, play on
Twelfth Night, (1602) William Shakespeare

Music has always been important to me. At the age of ten I joined the church choir and I stayed until my mid-thirties. I had a fair voice, so in a very short time I was singing most of the solos. Mike Spencer was my first choir master and would throw a hymn book at you if you misbehaved and then add, 'next time, it will be a piano'.

If you were singing well out of tune he would say, 'that was not just bad tuning boy, it was bad geography.'

Those were great days, when I was a boy soprano. We had a strong choir then and sang at most of the cathedrals and some of the churches in the south of England.

My favourite solo was *Hear My Prayer* by Mendelssohn (also known as *Oh for the Wings of a Dove*). It was recorded but we were always plagued by TV interference from the aerials at Crystal Palace. Fortunately, a member of our choir worked for the BBC, so he managed to clean up the recording. Sadly, one of my friends recorded over it.

As a boy soprano I attended a few courses, some local, some further afield and residential. At one residential course I found myself sleeping in a dormitory with some of the others from the course. The corridor had a highly polished floor and one of the boys found that it was good for sliding on with his woollen socks. He got faster and faster until he shouted, 'I'm coming!'

We saw him hurtling past the door, followed by a loud bang and a cry, as he hit the door at the end of the corridor. He came hobbling into the dormitory with holes worn in his new socks. That would have taken a lot of explaining when he got home.

Closer to home, I went on a course at Addington Palace. There was a huge Cedar Tree at the side of the building which we used to love climbing on. (More recently, I photographed a wedding at Addington Palace and noticed that the same tree has some of its branches propped up and has a big notice saying DO NOT CLIMB).

My church used to be in the diocese of Canterbury, and I had the great privilege of being confirmed by Archbishop Ramsey. The BBC also did a documentary called The Archbishop, which followed the life of none other than Archbishop Ramsey. My part in it was filmed during the induction of our new vicar. I later watched the documentary with my parents and was delighted to see myself singing in the choir. I was surprised to see my head filling the screen, while eating an enormous cream bun at the reception afterwards. They say that everyone is entitled to fifteen minutes of fame, I had ten seconds.

Meanwhile, when I was twelve, I auditioned for, and was given the part of Oliver in the school musical of the same name. I loved it and we got a good review from the Croydon Advertiser. I was then put forward by the school for a part in *Noye's Fludde*, a Trinity School production. Unfortunately, all the main parts had already been given to Trinity boys and I became understudy for Jafet, one of the sons. Despite my darkest wishes, nobody broke their leg or went under a bus, so I became a walrus in the chorus. I was a good walrus though, and I got the chance to sing at the Fairfield Halls. Nonetheless I became disenchanted with operatics.

Back in the church choir, our choir master, Mike Spencer told us a very amusing tale about his friend, Roy Massey, who was playing an organ recital at Croydon Parish church. The organ console could not be seen by the audience and it was a swelteringly hot day. So, none of the audience were aware that Roy was playing in nothing but his string vest and pants. At one point, Roy gave a flourish with his left hand and knocked a very old piece of music onto the floor. It separated into individual pages and Roy said to Mike, 'I know the start by heart, but I need page seven'.

Later that year, Roy was offered the position of organist at Hereford Cathedral. His successor at Croydon Parish Church was Michael Fleming, no relation to the chap who wrote the James Bond novels. I passed all of my chorister exams and became a red ribband deputy. Unfortunately, the head chorister wasn't much older than me, so I was only head chorister for one year. My voice should have broken at fifteen, but I promised to sing Ave Maria at my sister's wedding, by which time I would be well over sixteen. I kept my promise and my voice broke the following day. Fortunately, I was left with a reasonable bass voice.

In a few years I was singing most of the bass solos, but my proudest moment was when I was asked to sing narrator of The Passion at Easter. We wore the priest's robes and processed from the high altar towards the congregation. I was in the middle, with my friend Trevor to my left, singing the part of Jesus Christ and my friend Dave, to my right, singing the part of Pontius Pilate, the choir were the crowd. Palm Sunday was based upon Matthew's gospel, Good Friday was based upon the gospel according to John.

One year I opened the wrong copy, when my friend Dave realised, he whispered to me 'you are singing the wrong one'. Although my heart was pounding in my chest with panic, I calmly finished the sentence, genuflected, crossed myself, and continued with the right gospel. Talking at coffee afterwards, it appeared that nobody even noticed!

Another year, I became all operatic and dramatic when I sang a passage from the Bible, sometimes known as the *Rocks Rent,* 'and the graves opened, and the dead bodies appeared unto many.'

I think I woke up half of the congregation. You don't do that sort of singing at St. John's.

A member of our choir attended Cambridge University, where she met her future husband. They were married in the cathedral, which is very rare. It must have helped that they both got a first and his father was a Don. Our choir was invited and both King's College and another College choir were there too. There were so many of us that it was decided that we would sit in the choir stalls while the two Cambridge choirs occupied the first three or four front rows. The service was superb, and it was heavenly singing from King's College Cambridge. It was followed by the wedding breakfast in the great hall and the day ended the way you would expect in Cambridge: the couple left for their honeymoon on a tandem.

Chapter 5

'There's no business like show business.'
(Title of the song by Irving Berlin)

At the age of twenty-four I was dating Jacky and I was growing increasingly suspicious as to why she was never available on Friday evenings. She said she was rehearsing. So, one Friday I went with her. Sure enough, the Hillcrest Players were rehearsing a review called *Ruby's Garter*.

A few of the songs may have been bespoke but the majority were well known so I was singing enthusiastically from the auditorium. The next thing I knew, I was in the chorus and I had three cameo roles. They included Old Hezekiah, a 101-year-old prospector, Ed Pierce or Arrow Hat, and a gambler dressed all in black and wearing a gunslinger's belt and holster. I did one scene with the Chairman of Hillcrest Players, who gave me my first lesson in ad-libbing. He forgot his lines and bowled me a question, I couldn't think of what to say but Ed Pierce came to the rescue and said something very witty, making the audience laugh and putting the pressure back on him. After the show I apologised to John and he said something which has stayed with me all my life, 'if you need an ad lib, let the character speak for you.'

He will always be right, and this philosophy has served me well. The gambler had a fan club, but the average age was fifteen.

I enjoyed the show so much I was smitten. Sadly, the Hillcrest Players were a long way from home, and they were principally a drama group, so I joined the Streatham Hill Operatic Society. I did one show in the chorus and then to my surprise, I was offered a lead role of Robin Oakapple in Ruddy Gore and it was a fairly innovative production.

In the show there is a ghost scene which is traditionally played in the picture gallery. The director decided that the picture gallery would be closed for renovation and ghost scene played outside the gallery. Each ghost was dressed all in white and scrubbed with 'Daz', so they would be picked up by the ultraviolet light. They stood, each in their own archway, holding a heavy black curtain in front of them. When I approached each archway, the ghost dropped the black cloth. I knew what was coming, and I was scared. From an audience's perspective, the ghosts appeared from nowhere.

At this time, I was having problems with my landlady, so the director offered his spare bedroom. Back to the show, the director had the idea of us singing our verses of the patter song simultaneously.

Now he was a more experienced actor than I was, but he forgot that I was a trained chorister, so when he tried to stare at me while singing his verse, I just stared back and put him off instead. I had a car by then, so I was taking him home every night and Saturday was no exception. We were having a few drinks when he put his hand on my knee, and propositioned me whilst his wife was asleep upstairs. I have never been a violent man, but I was so affronted that I stood up and punched him hard, in the face, knocking him to the floor. I don't think I broke his nose, but to be honest I didn't hang around long enough to find out. I ran up to my room and locked the door.

It was lucky we had finished the show, because I left very early the next morning and drove home. I phoned his wife to thank her for her hospitality and to apologise for having to leave so early. Of course, I never mentioned the previous evening again.

When I returned to the society, he had left, so I stayed for a few more shows. This included The Boyfriend, in which I played Bobby Van Heusen. Jill, who played my partner, Maisie, was a dancer, so she taught me the Charleston, including the lift. The boy goes down on one knee while the girl runs at him. At the last minute the boy stands up and lifts the girl by the waist while she steadies herself with her hands on his shoulders.

All through the week, the best I could manage was to lift her just above ninety degrees, but on the last night I must have got the timing right because I lifted her vertically with her feet pointing at the ceiling. For a moment I thought I would fall over backwards, but I didn't, and she landed perfectly to rapturous applause. To my astonishment, after the show my father patted me on the shoulder and said, 'well done son.' This was the only time he ever said that.

Soon afterwards, and reluctantly, I left the Society and joined the Utopian Society who used the Lewisham theatre. This boasted a capacity of 1100 seats, a proper orchestra pit and professional stage and lighting crew. Altogether I played principal roles in about sixty shows at twelve theatres, but I am sure that neither you nor I have the time or patience to look at a veritable shopping list of the sixty shows. I have stuck to the most memorable.

I was cast as Woody Mahoney in *Finian's Rainbow* for South London Theatre Centre. It was a good part, in a great show and I learned a lot about acting.

I played 'Yamadori' in *Madam Butterfly*, for Opera Nova. It was a small part in a good production but, importantly, it was my introduction to Opera and my first opportunity to sing in Italian.

I once played Will Parker in *Oklahoma* on the Lewisham stage. It was most memorable for the audition. I did a good singing and dialogue audition and I was asked if I could tap dance. I said that I couldn't, but I had danced in other shows and I was a quick learner. A bit of a stretch, but as soon as I had learnt that I had got the part I bought some tap shoes and enrolled in a tap dancing class, to keep one step ahead of the game (forgive the pun).

By the time I played Freddie in *My Fair Lady*, I was the publicity officer for the Utopians and came up with the idea of contacting the agent of Mrs Gertrude Schilling to ask her to attend the Lewisham theatre wearing one of her son's hat designs. She agreed to come on Friday. We moved into the theatre on Monday and the following day we were burgled.

At that time there was a builder there and the theatre was left open all day. Why the dressing rooms were left unlocked is beyond me. It seemed more like sabotage than a burglary because the men lost only the top hats, the gloves and shoes and the ladies lost their costume jewellery. The society announced that they were not insured for personal losses, but amongst my losses was a black silk top hat which I had borrowed from a friend, called Chris Arden.

After the show it took me ages to find a suitable replacement. I finally found one which was better than the original, complete with its own box and brush set. It was expensive but my friend was very happy. I phoned the local newspaper and told them of our burglary. They were very sympathetic and published an article in the Thursday edition headlined 'The Show Must Go On'.

We opened on the Thursday evening without accessories and when we did the Ascot scene, we received a standing ovation. We managed to find replacement hats and gloves on Friday and Mrs Schilling came as promised wearing a very big hat. Unfortunately, she wore it throughout the performance and the poor people sitting behind her could hardly see a thing.

I also played Kipps, a dream of a part, in *Half a Sixpence*. As you are probably aware, the part of Kipps was originally played by Tommy Steele. With my publicity hat on, I discovered that although Tommy Steele is known as the, 'Bermondsey Boy', he was born in Catford, the same town as the Lewisham theatre. I wrote to his agent, not expecting a reply. To my surprise I received a letter from Tommy himself apologising that he was too busy to come but wishing us success with our show and enclosing a signed photograph of himself. I put both in one of the display cabinets outside the theatre.

I was once asked to audition for *The Pirates of Penzance*, for Medway Opera Company. They had lost their Pirate King six weeks before the show and someone had seen me playing the part before. Not only was it a pro-am production, it had a cast of sixty and was being performed at a very large theatre. For those of you who are not familiar with the term 'pro-am', it describes a production with professional principals and amateur chorus.

Sadly, my boss at the time hated amateur operatics. He couldn't understand why grown men would prance around on stage, wearing make-up. I think David Bowie and Alice Cooper would disagree. Nobody in my office was sick, or on holiday, we had little work to do and I had plenty of leave left. Despite this, my boss would not allow me to take any time off. I could call him a word beginning with 'b', and ending in 'd', but he doesn't resemble a bird, so I will leave it to your imagination.

Every day I had to commute by motor bike from Lewisham to Putney and back to Lewisham. When I arrived home, I had a quick shower, changed, and drove the thirty miles to Chatham and the theatre. By the end of the week I was running on pure adrenalin. On Friday I was joined by my wife, Sue, and her mother, and we got stuck in a traffic jam. It turned out to be a serious accident and we were stationary for some time.

It was before the day when we had mobile phones, so I couldn't inform the theatre. By the time we arrived, the orchestra had just started the overture. As I was in the opening scene, I was told to stand still while three ladies dressed me and put on my makeup and wig. I made it on stage just in time if I hadn't, I think they would have sued me – I had, after all, joined the world of the professionals.

In case you are wondering, the orchestra had to start when they did in order to finish before 10 p.m., in accordance with The Musicians' Union rules.

On Saturday, Sue came with me again. I did two shows and then we both went to the after-show party. When we left the party my adrenalin tanks must have been empty because I slept most of the way home. Even when we arrived home at 4 a.m., I swear I was asleep before my head hit the pillow. Sue was worried when she had to shake me to wake me up at 7 a.m. on Monday. My body had obviously decided that enough was enough and shut down completely. I had slept for twenty-seven hours.

I played the part of Melvin P Thorpe in the *Best Little Whorehouse in Texas* for Artform. It was a wonderful part in a great show, and I enjoyed it immensely. You would think that people who were easily offended would stay away from a show so named but they came, were offended and left early.

I joined Bromley Operatic Society to play Sir Arthur Sullivan in *Taran Tara! Taran Tara!* It was the story of Gilbert and Sullivan and their relationship with D'Oyly Carte. It was a great show and a privilege to play a real person.

I went on to play Mr Cellophane or Amos Hart in *Chicago* on the Churchill stage in Bromley. The Churchill theatre could be a fairly intimidating place with its eight-hundred-seat capacity and a stage which is fifty four feet wide, making it one of the biggest non-opera house stages in Europe. As you would expect, the Thursday matinee audience mainly comprises quietly appreciative retired ladies, but this audience were very quiet. Everyone kept returning to the dressing room saying that they thought the audience were asleep.

I was particularly worried because my song relied on audience reaction. I was about to learn the power of pathos. I ran on to the stage, delivering the soliloquy and had just reached the line 'no one ever listens to me, no one ever notices I'm around'. When a lady in the front row shouted, 'yes we do, poor little bugger.'

The rest of the audience erupted with laughter, and I felt a rush of adrenalin the like of which I have never felt. It shot up my spine to my brain and I gave the performance of my life. Tony Britton was rehearsing his show at the Churchill at the same time, so he watched some of our dress rehearsal. Afterwards he said, 'I had no idea that amateur shows could be so professional.'

I soon became the publicity officer for Bromley Operatic Society. When they did *West Side Story*, one Saturday, before the show, I arranged for two vintage Cadillacs to be parked on the pavement outside the theatre. I got the girls to dress in costume and adorn the cars.

Whilst I was a member of Bromley Operatic Society, I became good friends with one of the ladies in the chorus. One day she invited me to dinner along with several of her friends. I knew she was a vegetarian, so I assumed her friends were as well and was right. The entire meal was vegetarian, but her cooking was so good that I didn't miss meat once.

When I was complementing the host on her cooking, I happened to mention that I was normally a meat-eater. When the girl opposite me learned that I was a carnivore she started lecturing me on the virtues of being a vegetarian, which lasted throughout the meal. I soon became fed-up, so I asked her how long she had been a vegetarian.

'Two whole weeks' she said proudly.

What I said next was a bit of a 'faux-pas', but she had been preaching at me for over an hour and I couldn't help myself. I said, 'so, you didn't mind eating Bambi two weeks ago?'

There was a silence around the table and, as the meal was over, I felt it was time to leave. The following morning, I telephoned the host to thank her for hospitality and to apologise for my behaviour. She said that there was nothing to apologise for because she found the whole affair hilarious. I was never invited again, so I guess her friends found it less amusing.

I finally left Bromley Operatic Society because I was tired of the sort of politics which you often find in big societies. I joined Ferrier Operatic Society who use The Bob Hope theatre in Eltham. They are a very friendly society and I stayed to do several shows. I guess my favourite parts were Eisenstein in *Die Fledermaus* and 'Danilo' in *The Merry Widow*. Both shows are operas by Strauss and Lehar respectively. But we did the amateur versions.

I joined the Sevenoaks Opera Company and played Dancairo, in *Carmen* at the Stag Theatre. Although it was a relatively small part, I had the honour of singing with Karen Harper of English National Opera, and Victoria Simmonds, our other Carmen, who was discovered by ENO in that very production.

A few years after I had left Bromley, I returned to the Churchill to support another Society. It was a show I hadn't seen before and it was great. I knew most of the cast so after the show I thought I would go backstage to congratulate them. I tried to use the stage door but none of the codes I knew would work. The stage crew were enjoying a drink near the door, so I asked them for a code. He didn't know me, so he looked at the stage manager. The stage manager said, 'don't you know who he is? It's Mr Cellophane. Give him the code.'

It's nice to be recognised.

A show that is worth remembering was another production of *Die Fledermaus,* performed by Sevenoaks Opera Company at the Orchard theatre in Dartford. This time it was the professional version and I played the part of Dr Falke. It was a pro-am production with a strong principal line up and starred Nicholas

Parsons as Frank, the Prison Governor. It was a non-singing part, but it exploited his ability for ad-lib and comic timing. Another part of which I am proud was Tevye, in *Fiddler on the Roof*. Although it was a semi-staged production, to play the part made famous by Topol was a dream come true.

Of course, I must not forget, Mr Peacham in *The Beggar's Opera,* for Beckenham Theatre Centre as this is where I first met Liz.

She was helping with front of house and one night was sitting in the front row. I was sitting on the stage in a 'drunken stupor', slumped against the scenery and the actor playing Macheath, was lying on his front singing a ballad. The theatre was very intimate, so he decided to crawl forwards until his legs were on the stage and his arms were on Liz's lap. He looked into Liz's eyes and sang a verse of the ballad.

The production I think of as the show that was transformed from a trauma into a triumph was *Ruddigore,* for the Century Company at the Greenwich theatre. I was cast as Sir Despard, and the poor girl originally cast as 'Mad Margaret', was fraught with illness. In six months, we only rehearsed two or three times, so we hadn't built our characters or established a rapport. Eventually, just two weeks before the show, she had to withdraw. One, of the cast, had been to a professional production of *Ruddigore,* and said that Mad Margaret was excellent. The committee gave her permission to approach Alex to ask her to be our Mad Margaret. We didn't expect her to do an amateur show but to our surprise she said yes. She arrived, as promised, on the Saturday before the week. We had an all-day rehearsal, established a wonderful rapport and went on to do a splendid show. It was a baptism of fire, but she was a joy to work with. Sadly, she couldn't come to the party so none of us could say thank you.

Last, but certainly not least, I played the part of Sweeney Todd for The Bob Hope Theatre Company. It was probably the greatest, and definitely, the hardest part, I have ever played. Sondheim's music is often horrendously difficult to learn, but once mastered it is tremendously rewarding.

My friend, Sheila Arden, played a superb Mrs Lovett. Her comic and musical timing were outstanding, and I would like to think that we worked well together.

My barber shop was on top of an eight-foot-high cube and the crew built me a special chair. When I despatched a victim, I pulled a lever and the corpse slid through a trap door in the floor, landing on a mattress below. The blood was ingenious. Each victim wore a bag filled with stage blood inside their shirt with a clear plastic tube leading to their throat. At the vital moment, the victim squeezed the bag, and blood appeared to gush from the throat. It was gory but effective.

Brian, who played Pirelli, wanted to modify the tubing so he blocked the end and added holes along the side of the tube, taping it across his throat. He added more holes every night until one night, the tube split open and the blood squirted in all directions. It was effective but the audience were revolted.

We ran for two weeks with two days off in the middle. On the first Saturday my cousin Mike and his wife Bobbie came all the way from Litchfield, near Birmingham. I had given Mike an aisle seat on the pretext that he was very tall, and it would give him more leg room. But I had an alternative motive. During one of the songs I was asked to jump off the stage and attack the audience. I could come as close as I liked as long as I didn't touch. On the night of the show Mike and Bobbie, came I knelt in front of Mike, and I sang sweetly about my daughter who I would never see again. I then turned on Mike, put my razor under his bearded chin, looked into his eyes and said viciously 'all right you sir, how about a shave?'

I saw the look of terror in his eyes and leaped back onto the stage thinking 'mission accomplished'. In the bar after the show Mike said, 'for a moment I forgot you were my cousin'.

The following day I heard that my mother had died. I was devastated. When I was up to it, I phoned Sheila. She was so understanding saying that she would understand if I withdrew from the show but she would prefer me not to. I was not only close to my mother but was also her sole executor, so I drove all the way to Devon. I phoned Sheila the next day to say that I would return on Tuesday on three conditions; one, everyone was to treat me normally. Two, No one should offer condolences or mention my mum before the show. Three, I was to be given some time on my own before the show.

I arranged what I could on Monday and stayed one more night. When I returned to the theatre on Tuesday everyone was wonderful. Twenty minutes before the show I went down to an empty room, stared into one of the mirrors and let all of Paul Allen drain out of me and be replaced by Sweeney Todd. I continued this ritual every night. The show went very well but in the dressing room afterwards I completely broke down. It was as if the need to play Sweeney was holding me together, as soon as it was over, I fell apart.

The following day my mum would have attended the show.

The theatre had offered to re-sell the ticket because it was a full house, but I said the seat should remain empty. I dedicated the show to her and gave, what was arguably, my best performance. The after-show party was held on the stage and Brian led me up to my barber shop on some pretence or other. He tied me to the chair and announced, 'this is Pirelli's Revenge.'

Brian was a barber by trade, and he had straightened my naturally curly hair for the show. I looked more like Lou Ferrigno as the incredible hulk. He gave me a quick haircut, untied my bonds and pulled the lever; I plummeted through the hatch. The two members of the stage crew, who were waiting below, caught me and slid me along the floor. I burst through the trapdoor at the front of the cube and narrowly avoided landing in the orchestra pit. It was lucky that my girlfriend was there because I had a great deal to drink. It was probably a pressure release for the mixture of elation and grief that I was feeling. I dearly hope that one day I will play Sweeney Todd again but under happier circumstances.

Chapter 6

The show must go on

Shows, like life, don't always go according to plan, it is how you deal with the situation that matters. I have selected a few shows where something went wrong. Judge for yourself how well it was dealt with.

Once I was in a production of *The White Horse Inn* for the Utopians. The man playing Valentine Sutton had upset the stage crew. So one night, they set his suitcase as normal, but filled it with cast iron stage weights. When he tried to lift it, he said, 'oh it's too heavy. Have it, sent up.'

My first production with Ferrier was *Fiddler on the Roof* at The Trident Theatre Greenwich in which I played Motel the tailor and my friend, Len Thorpe, was Tevye.

In one scene Tevye came on stage pulling his milk cart because his horse had died. During one show a wheel fell off his cart. Tevye looked up to heaven and said, 'God you have taken my horse; now my cart is broken.'

Possibly the most disastrous show I was in was *The Mikado*, for Norwood Operatic Society. It was potentially a good show and I loved playing Pooh-Bah, but the person playing Ko-Ko was having considerable problems at work and hadn't learned his lines. If you shared the stage with him, you never knew what he was going to say next.

Pooh-Bah should have been a very easy character to

assimilate. However, I struggled with this character more than any other. This was partly because Ko-Ko was so difficult to act with but it also because I saw Pooh-Bah as a pompous fat man and couldn't seem able to transform myself into him in my imagination. This was a thought that I just couldn't shake and finally, the director asked the committee to hire me a fat suit. This they did, and as soon as I donned the fat suit something miraculous happened. Pooh-Bah suddenly arrived, complete with his walk, gestures superior sneer and voice.

One night when Ko-Ko was particularly bad, Poo-Bah sent him off. Nanki Poo and Poo-Bah then continued the scene, paraphrasing Ko-Ko's lines. Ko-Ko hadn't even learned his main song, the 'Little List' one where he reads out all the categories of people he thinks should be executed, so Pish-Tush snatched the scroll from him and completed the song. Unfortunately, the press couldn't see past Ko-Ko and the only headlines I remember were 'Ko-Ko was just so-so' and 'a weak cup of Ko-Ko'. What is even more sad is that it turned out to be Norwood's swan song as they never produced another show.

As Will Parker in *Oklahoma* my main song was Kansas City. When I sang the line 'they went and built a skyscraper', the male chorus would form a human pyramid. One night I forgot the line and one member of the chorus refused to start the pyramid. After the show he gave me a very hard time.

The next day I was paranoid, I went on the stage repeating the lines in my head. Once I had sung the line, I relaxed and lo and behold, skipped half a verse. When I came to what I thought was the end of the song I started my tap routine, I didn't recognise the music so I step-ball-changed and step-ball-shuffled across the stage until I recognised it again. I then did my tap dance and then stepped back to give the floor to the real dancers. I said to the person next to me, under my breath, 'what was the orchestra playing at?'

He replied 'don't you know? You've just missed half a verse'.

I must have gone as white as a sheet. In the bar after the show I was delighted when a friend came up to me and said how much he enjoyed my dance, 'but what were the orchestra doing?'

It taught me another valuable lesson; if you make a mistake, be confident and look innocent.

Bromley Operatic Society did a production of *The Pyjama Game* in which I played Hines, a time-and-motion man. I had to model a pair of pyjamas and demonstrate that if I breathed in very deeply the button would pop off. The pyjama bottoms then fell down, revealing some very leery stars-and-stripes boxer shorts. One day I forgot to put on the boxer shorts, unfortunately, it also had to be the day I was wearing the only posing pouch I possessed. Quite why I was wearing it escapes me, however I had to go through with dropping my trousers. The audience laughed much louder than ever before and when I made a rather 'cheeky exit' upstage, they were in hysterics. Afterwards the producer said, 'that was brilliant, keep it in.'

I hoped I had!

Bromley also did *My Fair Lady*. I was Freddy and my ex-wife, Sue, was Mrs Pearce, Higgin's housekeeper. Mrs Pearce had just shown Eliza up the stairs, only to find that the stage crew hadn't unlocked the bedroom door. She said, 'oh dear, the door is stuck again – must have it seen to. Eliza, let me show you to a different room.'

I performed in a production of *Orpheus* for Ferrier. The producer, Barbara Archer, directed me to rush off the stage disguised as a shepherd boy, remove my cloak and come back on singing, 'no shepherd I, the name is Pluto, the King of Hades.'

During the dress rehearsal, I rushed off and my cloak got caught on the scenery pulling the knot tight. I went back on the stage and sang, 'No shepherd I, the name is Pluto can't get his cloak off.'

To my amazement, the chorus echoed my words and sang, 'Pluto it is, can't get his cloak off.'

During the same show I gave my name to Jupiter played by Len Thorpe. He couldn't remember his lines, so he said, 'Pluto, what kind of name is that? Sounds like a dog.'

I bristled, folded my arms, glared at him and said, 'please don't take the mickey.'

During *Sweeney Todd* there was one scene where I had Pirelli shut in a trunk. He was unconscious rather than dead because I was interrupted before I could finish him off. One night I went to open the trunk to dispatch him, when he suddenly flew open the lid and knocked the razor out of my hand. I watched as the razor fell to the floor, eight feet below. With no weapon, I had few options, so I banged him on the head with my fist. This knocked him out long enough for me to run down the stairs and retrieve my razor. When I returned, I was able to finish him off.

The Centenary Company did a rarely performed Gilbert and Sullivan operetta, called *The Grand Duke*. I was Ludwig and I had four wives, sequentially, of course, to keep the show respectable. At one point my fourth wife was getting drunk on champagne, which she was drinking from the bottle. While I was trying to wrestle the bottle from her, she would back up three steps to the rostrum, pretend to trip and land on the chaise longue. One night she only backed up two steps and really tripped over the last step, landing heavily on the chaise and pulling me on top of her. Under our weight, the chaise started to roll, stopping within half an inch of the edge of the rostrum. She looked up at me and said, 'that went rather well.'

She didn't realise how near we came to be falling off the edge and landing in the orchestra pit.

I rarely withdraw from a show, but sometimes it is unavoidable. I was going through a mad, two-year period in my life, when I couldn't get enough of operatics. Barbara asked if I would audition for the Pirate King in *The Pirates of Penzance*, because Biggin Hill Operatic Society had held their auditions and were not successful in casting the Pirate King. When I said yes, she asked me if I would audition at the musical director's apartment. It transpired that he owned the south wing of Lullingstone Castle.

It was the most relaxed audition I have ever had. I was in a large, elegant room looking through a picture window at the lake. I imagined I was on the high seas. I got the part and I was enjoying rehearsing with the rest of the cast. At the same time, I was also rehearsing for the part of Strephon in *Iolanthe*, for Grosvenor Light Opera Company. During the first performance I developed a slightly sore throat which, by Saturday, was a severely sore throat.

As I was performing Pirates of Penzance in two weeks, I took the advice of a fellow principle and saw an ENT specialist based in Upper Wimpole Street. He normally only saw professional singers, so when he found out that I was an amateur, he reduced his fees from £90 to a mere £60 for a ten-minute consultation. It was worth it though, because he diagnosed an acutely ulcerated soft palate. He also said that if I didn't rest immediately, I could lose my voice forever. Consequently, I had no choice but to withdraw from *The Pirates of Penzance*. Fortunately, I found a friend, Colin who was free and had always wanted to play the Pirate King, he was able to master the part very promptly. I went to see the show to support him and the rest of the cast. It was a good show, but it felt a bit strange watching someone else playing my part.

After the show I went backstage to congratulate Colin, and, to my great surprise, the cast gave me a galleon in a glass decanter as a present. It has pride of place in my house and always will. After all, it is the only time I have ever received a gift for not doing a part!

Chapter 7

Friends in harmony

When I performed in *The Merry Widow* for Ferrier, the widow was played by Veronica Layne, 'Ronnie' to her friends. Soon after the show she approached me, asking if I would consider taking one of our duets 'Driving in the Park', from the show and entering it in the Beckenham Festival. I told her that I had not done any competitions before and I wasn't keen on the idea. She took one look at me and said, in her inimitable Glaswegian way, 'don't be such a wimp, you've got to do it.'

What could I do but obey?

On the day we sang well, but the competition was fierce; we were competing against fifteen other couples. The adjudicator read out the results in reverse order, and when he reached second place, I was sure he had left us out. I was wrong; we came first! I was amazed, but Ronnie wasn't surprised at all. The whole experience gave me a lot more confidence, so the following year I dared to enter a few solo classes.

Unbelievably, within a few years, I had won gold medals in opera, operetta, oratorio, old musicals, modern musicals and duets at Beckenham, Bromley, Blackheath and Croydon festivals.

One year I was lucky enough to win best in festival with Mr Cellophane. Another year I took part in the winner's concert at Fairfield Halls with Gliding from *Ragtime*. I was the only adult there and it was very humbling experience to watch a child play the organ with blocks of wood tied to his feet in order to reach the pedals. A few years later, I represented my church in an all church gospel choir with Graham Kendrick, a singer/songwriter of Christian songs of praise.

I first met Iona Jones when I sang the duet with Ronnie at Beckenham Music Festival. Iona had already taught Ronnie and asked if I would I like to come to her as well. In the intervening years she has become more than just a singing teacher; she is a valued friend, a confidant, she supports and encourages me and, inevitably she is a substitute mum.

She put together her 'dream team' of singers of which I was pleased to be a part. James Kinsella is a professional singer with a beautiful Irish tenor voice, Jean Low has a wonderful voice and is the only soprano I know who can float her top notes, Jackie Montgomery has a very pure voice and specialises in unaccompanied singing and Jo Begley has a fine voice and is also an accomplished comedienne. And then there is me; I sang 'a bit' of baritone and I loved to communicate with the audience.

Janet Bishop is our professional pianist and the best accompanist I have ever sung with. Iona compiles and compares each concert and joins us to sing each ensemble. She is a very elegant lady and her husband, John, is a quintessential gentleman.

We've performed several charity concerts together but the biggest one was at my church where we called ourselves 'Friends in Harmony'. We had several sponsors who covered the running costs and another company provided the wine for the interval. We played to a capacity audience of three hundred and, together with the raffle, raised £3,500.

Jo was playing the lead in a show at the Bob Hope Theatre, Eltham. When at the same time, finding himself with a few days off between filming, Jude Law decided to visit his parents who still live in Eltham. Jude and Jo had acted together in their youth, at the Bob Hope Theatre. He decided that while he was in town, he would revisit the theatre where it all began. He watched the show and afterwards, in the bar, when Jo came in, he greeted her like the old friend she was. As Jo said, 'that night, my street cred went up three-hundred percent.'

Adriano Graziani used to sing with us, until he took the brave step of leaving his day job and enrolling in The Royal College of Music. After the first year, I had the great delight of singing a duet with him.

During his second year, Kiri Te Kanawa was lecturing at the college and spotted his talent. When he left the college, she asked him to accompany her on a tour of Russia, sadly it was cancelled due to Kiri's ill-health.

In 2009 I joined Georg Torman's group who were rehearsing to sing pop carols at the Royal Albert Hall. We were called the London Concert Chorus and we sang with the London Concert Orchestra. We had six performances in December and one of them clashed with our friend's significant birthday. She invited us to join her at a restaurant and I figured that if Liz went straight there, I could make it after the performance. I made it just in time but had no time to change. Arriving in my dinner jacket, I think most of the other diners thought I was a waiter.

The next year I sang with Georg again. This time the numbers had swelled to a hundred and twenty. Georg started a Mexican wave during Slade's 'So Here it is, Merry Christmas'. The choir were very quick to catch on and some of the audience also joined in. By the end of the song, five thousand five hundred people, had joined us. It was one of the most emotional singing experiences I have ever had.

Chapter 8

Music to my ears

It is not all about me singing. I also enjoy listening to music at home and going to concerts, shows and operas.

I bought my first stereo at seventeen. It consisted of a Goldring GL78 record deck, a Metrosound ST60 amplifier (which looked more like a mixing desk because of its slider controls), and a pair of Wharfedale Glendale Speakers.

One Saturday evening, I invited my friends, including the vicar's daughter, to listen to some records. It was getting late, so the vicar came to collect his daughter, he banged on the door loudly and rang the bell. My father was furious, so he flung open the window and bellowed 'who the hell is that?'

'I am the vicar of St John's and I have come for my daughter.'

My father replied, 'I don't care who you are, no one wakes me up at midnight.'

My dad then strode into my bedroom and told me to return Charlotte to her father. I did, and without a word, the pair of them disappeared into the darkness. It was a natural conclusion to our evening, so my friends bid their farewells'. I was dreading choir the following day, but nothing was said.

The next year, I moved into my first rental flat and I decided to upgrade my speakers. My friend, Chris Rogers, designed me a pair loosely based on the Kef concerto. He designed the internals and the crossover circuit boards, and although they took a while to build, they sounded superb.

A few years later I built another pair. This time they were a Chris Rogers published design for a domestic monitor speaker and were available in kit form from a retail outlet.

For my twenty-second birthday I decided to have a big party. I made some party tapes, I had an Aiwa cassette deck and my speakers were complete, although not veneered. I had hired the church hall and because I thought that my amplifier was not good enough, I asked Chris if he could lend me one. He lent me a two-box Harmon Kardon amp. Adding, as I left his flat, 'sorry I can't make your party but look after the amp'.

'I always look after your things; why single out this one?' I asked.

'Because it has to go back, and it is worth two grand,' he replied.

I nearly fell down the stairs, two thousand pounds is a lot for an amplifier now, but back then it was a fortune. The party went with a swing and the sound was superb. Soon after, I upgraded my amplifier to an AR Cambridge. Then, I bought my first flat and went mad, buying a Linn LP 12 record deck, followed by my first valve amp. It was wonderfully warm and detailed, but it proved to be unreliable.

At this stage, I met Mark. I went to a Linn presentation where they said that they had two systems behind some screens. They played some unknown music on both systems and asked which one was best. Ninety percent of the room said the second system was best and nine percent said system one. Mark was the only one who said they were both the same. The Linn representative said that Mark was the only person in the room who got it right. He added that the demonstration was to show that when choosing a system, it is vital that you listen to some music that you know very well.

Mark and I became friends, not only because of our shared liking of good hi-fi, but because we both liked real ale and curry. He also introduced me to John, a fellow hi-fi enthusiast.

In 1990, I moved to Chislehurst and Mark told me that John was selling his hi-fi system. Mark had already offered to buy his speakers and John had a buyer for his record deck, so I bought his amp. It sounded dreadful. Mark explained that it was a compatibility problem, explaining that very few speakers suited the Naim amp, except Linn or Naim. I reluctantly sold my speakers and bought a pair of Linn Saras. Reluctantly because once I had veneered my speakers, they looked superb.

The fact that I sold them and made a hundred pounds profit, sweetened the pill. The buyer didn't haggle over the price, so I agreed to deliver them to North London. This was no small achievement as each speaker was one metre high and weighed over 50 K.

Soon enough, CDs began taking over, so I bought a Marantz CD94 MK2. I then made the biggest mistake of my life. I bought an expensive, customised digital to analogue converter (DAC) for my Marantz. The upgrade involved the company altering some wires inside the CD player, so it could no longer work on its own. The unit worked brilliantly on another system but didn't work very well on mine, so I sold it, at an enormous loss, in favour of a Linn Karik CD player and a Linn Numerik DAC. Once my system was all Linn and Naim, it sounded excellent.

I now have about 300 CDs, ranging from Bach to the

Beatles, Elgar to Enya and Puccini to Pink Floyd. So, as you can see my collection is very eclectic.

To change the subject entirely, I once went to my church to hear Carlo Curley, an American organ virtuoso, giving a recital. Carlo came hours early to practice on St. John's organ which, as Adrian explained, was a magnificent instrument, it was in desperate need of repair with several of the keys having air leaks, causing a slight delay. Carlo ran his fingers over the keys, noting the delays, then played some major organ works perfectly. Adrian was both impressed and annoyed; it took Carlo ten minutes to achieve what Adrian had taken years to master. From an audience point of view, you never would have known there was anything wrong with the organ.

When Carlo had finished the recital, he told us an amusing story about when he entertained the local townswomen's guild, in the village hall of a small town in America. The hall had its own pipe organ, but it was covered with dust and nobody knew how to operate it. While he was cleaning it, he discovered that it could be played automatically, so he loaded it with a piece of Bach. Halfway through his recital he switched the organ to automatic and out came a major organ work of Bach, which he smugly pretended he was playing. He gave a flourish with his right hand, a flourish with his left, then a flourish with both hands and, standing up, he exclaimed, 'hi girls!'

At last, St John's organ was restored. The console was completely renovated and relocated to its original position on the opposite side of the chancel, the pipes were individually restored to remove the mellow sound that the Victorians so loved. When the work was completed the organ sounded terrific, but it cost an outrageous £150,000.

I saw Carlo Curley again, playing his touring organ at the Fairfield Hall. It was sublime. The touring organ consisted of a three-manual, electronic keyboard which resembled a church organ console, a set of dummy organ pipes and 400 speakers. Although Carlo's touring organ was technically portable, it needed a large lorry to transport it. Carlo admitted that his organ would never be the same as a church organ, but it was very close.

Another time. I went to the Royal Albert Hall with Adrian Adams and Mike Spencer, both my Church choir masters, to see Carlo Curley play duets with Roy Massey. Carlo was playing his touring organ whilst Roy was playing the Royal Albert Hall organ. It was the best organ recital I have ever heard in my life.

Roy came to see us after the recital. He said that when they first asked him to play a duet with Carlo Curley the chance to play the Albert Hall organ, was too good to miss, but playing duets with a brash American didn't appeal. When he met Carlo, however and heard him play he realised that he was not only a true virtuoso, but also a genius.

To show how varied my taste in music is, the next time I went to the Royal Albert Hall was to listen to Emerson, Lake and Palmer playing progressive rock. Years later, I went with my sister to see Cliff Richard. I also, went to the old Wembley Stadium to see Pink Floyd. It was fascinating to see that the capacity crowd consisted of three generations, such is the wide appeal of Pink Floyd. I also went to see many other concerts including, orchestral, jazz and folk.

I used to work for the Metropolitan Police Service (MPS), who had a branch known as 'the cab office'. Their principal responsibility was licensing London's black cabs. They also received short-notice complimentary tickets for West End shows that were not sold out. Any member of MPS could receive these tickets for a £1 admin charge. Courtesy of the cab office, I saw Dennis Waterman in *Windy City*, Noele Gordon (Meg Richardson from Crossroads) in *Call me Madam*, Elaine Paige in *Sunset Boulevard*, *Martin Guerre* and *Children of Eden*. The last show closed prematurely because it opened during the London bombings. Tourists were staying away from London and any shows without the benefit of advance bookings were doomed to failure. It was a pity, because I enjoyed *Children of Eden* so much that I saw it twice.

I paid to see *Phantom of the Opera* starring Dave Willetts, *Starlight Express* and *Les Miserables* starring Colm Wilkinson and Michael Ball. I thought *Les Miserables* was so good that I saw it another two times. I also saw *Miss Saigon* in the West End and the Broadway version of *The Pirates of Penzance* at the Wimbledon Theatre.

My wife Liz, and I went to see *The Beautiful Game* courtesy of my company and we saw *Anything Goes* at Drury Lane, courtesy of one of my wedding clients, who was working at the Theatre Royal.

I went with my wife and a few friends to the Royal Opera House to see Sweeney Todd, starring Sir Thomas Allen. As you would imagine, it was a highly professional but very sanitised production. During the interval, while we were enjoying a glass of champagne, I saw Stephen Sondheim, the writer of the show. I wanted to rush up to him and tell him how much I admired his work, especially having played three of his principal roles.

I refrained, because he is a very solitary man and may have resented the intrusion.

Being in the Royal Opera House, I remembered a story once told to me by John, a musical director I used to work with. He worked for Dame Joan Sutherland whenever she was in the country. One year, she was booked to sing an opera at the Royal Opera House with Luciano Pavarotti. On the opening night, they overheard Pavarotti boasting to the press that he was the most powerful tenor in the world and no soprano could match him. Dame Joan decided to teach him a lesson.

That night John sat in the front row, full of anticipation. When they sang their first duet, Dame Joan ended on a top A and Pavarotti was supposed to end beneath her. Instead, as if to prove a point, he soared up to a top C as loud as he could, overpowering Dame Joan. John saw a glint in her eye, and she put one foot forward into a ballet position, which was a sure sign that something magical was about to happen. She zoomed up to a top E, which she sang so loudly that she obliterated Pavarotti and made the chandeliers swing. Pavarotti never again tried to upstage her.

Over the years, I have been to see numerous amateur shows. These include *The King and I*, *Hello Dolly*, *South Pacific*, *Pirates of Penzance*, *Camelot*, *Chicago*, *Tarantara Tarantara* and *42nd Street*.

A wise producer once said, 'there should be only two differences between a professional production and an amateur one – one, the professionals have a bigger budget for costumes and scenery, two, amateurs don't get paid.' Apart from the chosen few dozen at the top of their game, professionals are not very well paid. It is hardly surprising therefore, that many gifted amateurs choose not to pursue that path.

Finally, we come to operas. I have been to many pro-am productions, including *The Pearl Fishers*, *Aida* and *Madame Butterfly*, with my friend James Kinsella playing the leading role, and *The Masked Ball* and *Pagliacci*.

The only professional opera I have seen was *Rusalka*, by Dvorak at the Glyndebourne Festival. Jo Begley's company did some work for Glyndebourne every year, so were given a pair of complimentary tickets for the festival. One year, her boss couldn't go so he gave the tickets to Jo, she received them gratefully, but a few days later she realised she had a family commitment. She offered the tickets to me and I said yes, with thanks.

Neither Liz, nor I, had been to Glyndebourne before, so we cancelled all our commitments in order to be free to go. On the day, we arrived very early and because it was such a glorious day, we spread our picnic lunch next to the lake. It was a tradition to have half your picnic before the opera and half during the interval.

Later on, another small group laid out their picnic near us. We assumed it was a daughter with her elderly parents and when they spoke, they sounded upper middle class. They didn't talk to us before the opera but kept their own silence. The opera was very good, sung in its original Polish, with English subtitles. The singing was so heavenly that I was listening to the voices and only referred to the subtitles to keep up with the plot.

During the interval, we had more in common with the other family, so they started talking to us and the mother proudly announced that she had recently celebrated her eighty- eighth birthday. Later, the daughter was taking a photograph of her parents by the lake. Liz offered my services as I was a photographer. I was taking the three of them and somehow it must have slipped out that I was a wedding photographer.

The mother said that her granddaughter's wedding had been the highlight of her year and asked, 'do you have the same problem as my granddaughter's photographer struggling to get your clients to smile? Our photographer kept asking us to say cheese and none of us found the word remotely funny.'

I said, 'I quite agree with you madam. I prefer to use a rather more risqué word.'

Before I could finish, the mother asked, 'Do you mean f**k?'

Liz grabbed my arm and whispered, 'Did she just say what I think she said?'

I whispered back 'I'm afraid so.'

Her daughter looked mortified and, grabbing her mother's arm, said 'no he didn't mean that particular word', then looking at me added 'did you?'

I don't know how I kept my composure, but somehow I managed to say, 'no madam; that would be completely the wrong vowel sound. I prefer to use the word sexy.'

We made our apologies, gathered up our picnic things and headed for the car, laughing under our breath. When we reached our car, the car park resembled a posh car showroom. There were no decadent cars like a Ferrari or Lamborghini, but there were Rolls Royces, Bentley's and Jaguar's, Daimler's Maserati, Mercedes and even the odd Aston Martin. I was relieved that our car was a Mercedes, albeit 10 years old.

When we were walking back in to hear the second half, we were reflecting on how lucky we were. Not only were the tickets hard to come by, they were £150 for the cheapest seat; we were in a box.

The second half was as good as the first and we blissfully made our way home on a beautiful summer's evening. The weather had apparently been the best they had experienced in ten years. Rusalka was eventually chosen as the 'best in festival'. The leading lady had fallen off the stage only three days after we saw her and was replaced by her understudy for the rest of the run. We had paid nothing for the tickets, and we came away with a story to dine out on for years.

Chapter 9

It's a family affair

(Song sung by Sly & The Family Stone)

My father and I were never very close. This is probably partly because he was a chain smoker and from a fairly early age, I became an anti-smoker. When I was very young, I thought I was car sick, but my mother and I soon worked out that it wasn't the car making me sick, it was dad smoking.

A few years later he took up yoga. His favourite relaxation technique at home was to stand on his head, in front of the fire, while smoking and watching the television upside down.

My most vivid memories of my dad were not smoke-related, however. When I was in my mid-teens, Dad was an archery instructor. I joined his class because I thought it would help me to get closer to him, it didn't. Of all the students, I was the only one he completely ignored.

My next door but one neighbour, Graham, had a Wolseley 1500 which he couldn't afford to run. Our front garden was much bigger than his so he asked my dad if he could park on the drive. When I turned seventeen, he offered me the car at a very reasonable price. It had been on the drive for six months and was in no one's way because it was at the end of a very long drive. I was on the point of buying it when my dad said, 'if you buy it, you can get it off the drive.'

I could afford the car, but not the tax and insurance necessary to park on the road. Reluctantly, I had to let the car go.

At eighteen, he 'invited' me to leave home. I was shocked, but found a flat, in short measure.

When I was in my early twenties, I was at home doing some maintenance on my bike, while my dad was doing some major work on his car, assisted by my brother-in-law, Phil. I was fairly good at mechanics by this time, and I could see, from ten feet away, that he was trying to put the cylinder head on the wrong way around. I tried to point this out, but he told me to shut up and mind my own business. A few minutes later, after a lot of cursing and swearing, Phil suggested, probably more diplomatically than I, that he try the head on the other way around. Surprisingly, it fitted easily.

I used to think that I was the only one Dad didn't like, until I spoke to my older brother, Dave. He said that he and Dad had regular arguments and occasional fights.

When I was thirty, I heard that dad was selling the house, which he had, long since, bought from the council. I put in a full-price offer, which he accepted, and I put the matter in the hands of a solicitor. A few weeks later, the estate agent, who was a friend of my dad's, suggested that he put the house back on the market for more money. My dad did as Gordon said, but failed to inform me. I had to hear the news from my solicitor.

My dad's body was found next to the phone. He had had a heart attack. Twelve people had made offers on the house but each one had withdrawn their offers. My dad had only been retired for three months and he never saw the house sell.

The house took a year to sell and only raised an extra £5,000. I can't help thinking that, if dad had not put the house back on the market, he would still be alive today. I was much closer to my mum, although when I was younger, I must have caused her a lot of anxiety. I was continually arguing and fighting with my younger brother. I'm sure that she was proud of me when I joined the church choir, but she rarely saw me, because my father had to drive her. For a year after I left home, she invited me to Sunday lunch every week, much to my father's dismay.

When my father retired, they bought a Park home near Honiton in Devon, but my father died before they were due to move. My mum was faced with the difficult decision of whether to go to Devon on her own. I drove Mum down to Honiton to meet the neighbours. The site owner, Mr Nation, was very reasonable and said that if she decided not to go to Devon, he would buy it back. The neighbours were all very nice. They were all about the same age and retired and all promised to look after her. As a family, we agreed to support her if she decided to move down, which she did.

She employed a bricklayer to build a brick threshold under the home; this completed the home and hid the wheels. He also built a concrete slab path around the home. She had the garden landscaped and bought a shed. The home was called The Alpine Lodge because of its overhanging roof and the timber-beamed ceilings. She was proud of her home and rightly so, it was the biggest home on the site and featured three bedrooms, two bathrooms, a loft, a fully fitted, oak kitchen, a twenty- five foot, by fifteen foot lounge, and all new furniture.

One day Aunty Ruby came to stay. Her first words were, 'my, I had no idea how nice your caravan was. It's almost as big as my bungalow.'

Mum hated her park home being called a caravan, so she said, 'actually, Ruby, I think you'll find that it's a little bit bigger than your bungalow'.

Mum adapted very quickly to the Devonshire pace of life, she soon discovered the word, 'directly' which really means 'eventually' in Devon. On one visit, when Sue and I first arrived, Mum offered us a cup of tea, which she would do 'directly'. Two hours later we were parched and still waiting for our tea.

The house had to be painted every three years, so in the seven years that she lived there, I painted it twice. On the first occasion, I was up the step ladder painting and talking to Mum. As I started coming down the steps, I didn't realise that the paint pot had caught on the guttering. The pot tipped, the paint poured on my head. I shut my eyes quickly to avoid getting paint in them and when Mum had stopped laughing, she went to look for a towel. She was gone a long time and I knew exactly what she was doing. She was sorting through the towels to see which one she didn't mind being covered in paint! When she finally returned, I wrapped my head in the towel and Sue led me to the nearest bathroom. I took off my clothes, jumped in the bath and showered the paint off my head. When I was clean, I decided to call it a day.

Long before Mum left South Norwood, she passed her driving test and bought a little car. In Devon, it gave her the freedom to visit her favourite seaside resorts and garden centres. She also did meals on wheels, worked in a charity shop and joined the local skittles team. Mum developed a great sense of humour and often had me in stitches. One night we took her to a posh restaurant and she said she was 'Mrs Bouquet' (Bucket), from the television programme. She also said that we had come to sample their candlelight suppers. Fortunately, the waiter had seen some 'Keeping up Appearances' on TV, so he went along with the masquerade.

One year, we took her to my friend's villa in Ibiza. We showed her our favourite places and restaurants and afterwards she said it was the best holiday she had ever had.

It turned out to be the last holiday she ever had. She died at only seventy. The only consolation that I have is that she was with her friends on a trip to Bristol. She had just sampled her favourite tipple, sherry, at the Harveys Winery and was walking along the towpath when she suffered a massive heart attack and died instantly. At her funeral, it is silly, I know, but I couldn't help but think how much Mum would have enjoyed the day. The sky was blue, and the flowers were beautiful. The family agreed that because she had spent the happiest seven years of her life in Devon, she should remain there. Her ashes were buried in Exeter Crematorium, between two men, as she would have liked. The grounds were very well kept, and they hold a family service every year. Mum died over twenty years ago, but I still miss her dearly.

While I was still living with Mum and Dad, I was very grateful that Mum did all my washing. However, one day she left one of my thermal vests in the tumble dryer for too long. When it came out, I realised the disastrous effect excess heat had on thermalactyl. It was stiff as a board and small enough to fit action man!

Although there were ten years between my brother Dave and I, I suppose I looked up to him as a hero. For a few years we shared a bedroom, during which time he made me a superman costume. I made my maiden flight off his feet, I enjoyed flying for one second, but instantly realised I wasn't invulnerable. I hit the wall and it hurt. I split my new costume and that was the end of superman.

Dave formed a jug band, which I used to love listening to. He also joined the fire brigade and when he was on the appropriate shift, he would take me to school on the back of his motorbike.

At nineteen, he left home and went on a tour around the world. He got as far as Holland and fell in love with a Dutch girl named Siska. It was a very short world tour! They got married and had two beautiful girls, called Petroushka and Natasha. I used to go to Holland quite often. When I was young, I went with my parents, but when I was a bit older, I went on my own by train. In my late teens and twenties, I visited Dave on my motorbike.

Before Dave left the UK, he passed his driving test and sent his driving licence to Swansea for his full licence to be added. The DVLA made a big mistake and also added the code which allowed him to drive an HGV. He made the most of his luck, as one of his friends in Holland taught him to drive his Mercedes truck with a trailer.

His friend turned out to be an excellent teacher and Dave was a good driver and a very fast learner, so when he was competent, he applied to his friend's company for a job. The boss gave him a test and looked at his driving licence, not knowing that he should have had an HGV certificate- and that is how he became a medium-distance driver.

Once, he took me on a trip to Germany. He was fully loaded, so he had taken a long time to build up his speed. Up ahead, a Volkswagen Beetle was hogging the fast lane and Dave couldn't help but drive so close that the Volkswagen nearly disappeared, but he still wouldn't move over. Dave's air horns were from a railway train, so when he blasted them, the car moved out of the way so fast it was as if the driver had just woken up.

A few years later, Dave had been driving for several hours and he fell asleep at the wheel. He was in town and ran into another truck. Luckily for him he slumped across the bench seat. When he woke up, some scaffolding poles had come through the windscreen and were pinning him to the seat. The other driver was driving illegally because he had overhanging scaffolding poles with no flags or signs, so Dave won the insurance case. However, it affected his confidence so much that he had to leave the firm.

Instead, he fell back on the qualification that he got at Art College and became a graphic designer for a big printing company. A short time later, the company won the contract with 'Looney Tunes', the company who were responsible for producing the static merchandise for *Bugs Bunny* and *Tweety Pie*.

Several years later Dave became their head designer and he worked exclusively on the Looney Tunes contract. One day he discovered corruption in the company but when he reported it, instead of being rewarded, he was sacked. When the contact from Looney Tunes found out that Dave had left the company, he phoned Dave at home. He told Dave that he liked his innovative designs and the contract was due to be renewed. He said to Dave that if he could organise the production, the contract was his.

One year, Dave and Siska invited me to stay over Easter. I loved going to Holland, so I didn't hesitate and accepted. When I arrived, I was surprised to find that Dave had started raising chickens. He had bought twelve fertilised chicken's eggs and made an incubator. He had also bought a goose egg. It was lovely to see them hatch but hatching on Easter day made it all the more special. The goose must have felt left out because it also hatched but it was premature, and her legs were not strong enough to support the weight of her body. The chicks must have realised because they all rallied around her to support her.

When I returned the next year, the chicks had become chickens and the gosling was a very fine goose. The chickens followed the goose everywhere, probably identifying her as their mother. The goose was very protective of the chickens and, if anyone but Dave went near them, she became very aggressive. Dave said, 'why should I buy a guard dog when I have a guard goose?'

I visited Dave that year and he agreed to be my best man. Sadly, he died before he got the Looney Tunes contract, and before my wedding took place. He was only thirty-eight and I was devastated. His girls were only teenagers and far too young to lose their father. I went to the funeral with my parents and I insisted on seeing the body. I wish I hadn't because the Dutch don't believe in using make- up. So, his face was ash grey. It wasn't Dave, and it was very upsetting.

Now we come to my favourite sister Janet; she was my only sister, but she was still my favourite. When she left Selhurst Grammar school she went to secretarial college and then joined Croydon Council. She was very fast at typing and shorthand, so she soon became secretary of the Deputy Head of Croydon Council. At 21 she left home and married Phil at my church. I sang Ave Maria at her wedding. They started married life at Maidstone but soon moved to East Grinstead.

While they lived there, they had a neighbour who used to be a royal groom. He told us a story over dinner which he claimed to be true. He had just finished preparing a fine black stallion for the Queen Mother to inspect. Halfway through the inspection the horse broke wind. He was very embarrassed, so he said, 'I'm terribly sorry Mam.'

Allegedly the Queen Mother said, 'that's quite alright, I thought it was the horse!'

Phil was a town planner which is probably why I became a civil engineer. Years later, he got a job with the Hong Kong government. They were out there for 6 years, with a break in the middle. I used to love riding in his MG Midget, and we would often go out drinking.

They moved to Little Chalfont, near Amersham, in Buckinghamshire. Jan was the consummate hostess, so I used to enjoy visiting them. Jan had two boys while they were in Hong Kong. I used to enjoy playing, 'Uncle Paul', and when Tim was older, we used to play games. Phil boarded and carpeted the loft and put a snooker table up there. I wasn't aware that there were areas of the loft that were carpeted only, with no boarding. Tim and I were playing a game of snooker, when I stepped back to take my shot, and my leg went through the bedroom ceiling. I must have looked a sight from down below, with my leg dangling; the ceiling was a mess.

Years later, I rode to their house on my Suzuki GS850. It was being tuned by an ex-motorbike racer, so it was going very well. Tim wanted a ride on the back, so I obliged. Jan wanted a ride too. I thought that she was a seasoned pillion because she used to date one of Dave's friends who was a biker. Had I known that she had never been on his bike, I would not have gone so fast. On the way back she was thumping my back and I thought she wanted to go faster...so I did. When we got back to her house, she was shaking and said she would never go on a bike again.

Ever since I have known my brother-in-law, Phil, he has always been a keen runner and has been a member of one harrier club, or another. He has run the London Marathon every year since it started and his personal best time is three hours, which is very fast for an amateur. One year, Mum was already living in Devon, she hosted Christmas for us. We were all astonished when Phil announced that he was going for a run on Boxing Day, and we were less than sympathetic when he returned having been bitten by a farmer's dog.

His next birthday was his fortieth, and he was doing triathlon events. I was making novelty cakes at the time, so I made him an oval birthday cake. It depicted a swimming pool surrounded by an oval running track. In the pool was a swimmer, on the running track was a cyclist and a runner - being chased by a dog. Fortunately, Phil saw the funny side of it.

My two nephews have done very well for themselves. Tim, became an avionics engineer for British Airways. One day he was asked to repair the electronics of the plane's main door, he was just gluing the rubber seal back on, when they allowed the passengers back on the plane. An old lady asked what he was doing, and he said,

'Don't worry madam, I've just finished gluing the door back on!'

Nick got a degree in psychology. He is also interested in music. Sadly, Phil and Jan got divorced. It came a as shock to me as I thought their marriage was idyllic – obviously not.

Jan was always very thoughtful and generous in her choice of gifts, but for my fortieth birthday she excelled herself and bought me a flying lesson in a helicopter.

We flew over Leeds Castle and I proved to be more of a photographer than a pilot. I handed the controls back to the instructor and took pictures of the castle instead. Just before Jan's next significant birthday, she started having golf lessons, so I surprised her at her workplace with a set of ladies' golf clubs. I also made her a cake, depicting one hole of a golf course.

A few years later Jan met Roger. I was delighted when she asked me to give her away at her wedding, naturally, I also took some photographs.

A member of Roger's family agreed to buy my wine-making equipment, including twelve demijohns. I was trying to fit everything in my car and in my haste, I left my suit hanging in the hall. When I discovered that I didn't have my suit I thought of buying another one but when the landlord of the pub where Nigel and I were staying found out, he offered me his M & S suit, which he had just had cleaned. Unfortunately, Nigel told everyone, and all day I endured comments such as 'nice suit' and 'where did you get the suit?' Apart from that, the wedding went very well.

Ironically, just as Jan and I were closer than ever, she and Roger emigrated to France for a quieter pace of life. Roger's only worry was, what if he hit a cow when he was practising his golf swing? It is a lovely place to visit but it is 500 miles away. Tim also moved, to Northern Ireland, and Nick moved to Australia. All of them however have visited me in hospital and Jan comes quite often, despite the distance.

For one of Jan's significant birthdays, Liz and I were planning to go to France. I received a phone call from Roger to ask if I would join her friends in a surprise sing along of Cliff Richard songs. When we went to France, I managed to have a secret rehearsal with her friends, and we added some French songs too. On the day, Nick joined us to play keyboard.

My brother Nigel was only five and a half years younger than me, but we were two very different people, so we never got on. He did have his funny moments though. Our next-door neighbour, Gwen, was always swearing at her two girls and Nigel would sometimes eavesdrop. One day, Nigel went up to mum and said, 'you're a bugger, in fact you're a couple of buggers!'

For some strange reason, one Christmas, Mum and Dad bought us two joint Christmas presents. The first one, was a train set. Dad had mounted it on a board, with GPO button switches to operate the electric points. In one unfortunate moment, Nigel decided to put his arm across all of the buttons together. The points shorted and the track caught fire. That was the end of the train set. They also bought us a Scalextric set; Nigel spent all of his time breaking the cars, and I fixed them.

As Nigel grew older, he developed quite a dry wit. Dad was very skinny, showing all his ribs. The next-door neighbour had a very big, German Shepherd, called Caleb. The two things are connected – I shall explain. One day, dad was sunbathing in the garden when Nigel saw him, he shouted, 'quick Mum, call Dad in. Caleb might think he's a bone!'

At that moment Caleb jumped over the fence and Dad ran and hid in the shed. On a separate occasion, on the day Mum moved to Devon, I went into the loft to empty it. I shouted down to her, 'do you want to take the pouffe?'

I meant the thing you rest your feet on. Before Mum could answer, Nigel said, 'well I'm not staying here.'

Nigel's first job was at Berman and Nathan, theatrical costumers. He dressed some famous actors, including Sir Derek Jacobi and Michael Jayston. He occasionally worked for TVS, and they would send a limousine for him. While he worked at Bermans, I borrowed two hats, one for Pooh-bah in *The Mikado* and one for Sigismund in *The White Horse Inn*.

When Mum moved to Honiton, Nigel moved to Exeter to be fairly near to her. When Mum died, he moved to Hove. Mum's family was fairly small and, it's even smaller now. I loved my Nan and Granddad. Granddad used to wear a pair of hearing aids, if Nan was nagging him, he turned them off, and would then sit reading his newspaper in blissful silence. He used to smoke roll-up cigarettes, which he rolled by hand using very little tobacco. He would often fall asleep in his favourite armchair with the shrivelled excuse for a 'fag' hanging out of his mouth, dropping ash all over his clothes. Sometimes he would wake with a start, stand up and brush the ash all over the floor, leaving poor Nan to clear it up.

Granddad died when I was only 10. When I was told, I remember hiding behind the settee, so no one could see me crying. My Nan lived into her 90's, but it was still sad when she passed away.

My great aunt Nancy was an inspiration. When I was first married, she must have been in her late eighties, yet she was sitting on the floor with everyone else doing the row-boat song. When she was ninety, and staying with Sue and me, we took her to a restaurant to celebrate. She would wait until the waiter was next to me and then lean over to pinch his bum. The first time he looked at me angrily, the second time he looked less angry and by the third time he was blowing me kisses. I tried to explain that it was Nancy and not me, but the waiter wouldn't believe that an elderly lady would display such behaviour.

The next Saturday we took her to Devon. She thought that I was taking her home to Bristol. Little did she know that Mum had arranged a surprise party for her. She was sprightly until she was ninety-three, when she had a fall and broke her hip. Sadly, she never recovered and died at ninety-four. I think that if she had not had that fall, she would have lived until she got a telegram from the Queen. She had a wonderful philosophy for getting old. She used to say, 'you are not old until you start acting your age.'

The only uncle on my mum's side was Uncle Frank. He took one look at me when I was born and emigrated to New Zealand. He obviously, didn't like what he saw. He married a Kiwi called Pauline and had two children. Sadly, he died, but I did meet his wife Pauline and my two cousins, Chris and Debbie, when they came to the UK for a visit back in the 1970s. I took Pauline to see a show in London on the back of my motorbike, it was great.

Chris has been over twice since then, once with her partner, Robyn, to see me in hospital. Chris was very good at rugby and went on to represent New Zealand as an All Black. My cousin Mike took great pride in telling his friends at his rugby club that his cousin Chris was an All Black, they made the same mistake that you probably have. Chris is not short for, Christopher, it is short for Christine. The New Zealand ladies' rugby team was also called, All Blacks, and performed the Haka before the start of every game. Sadly, the New Zealand government made them change their name and they were forbidden from doing the Haka. However, Chris was an 'All Black' when they won the World Cup, and I am very proud of her.

On my father's side, my granddad died long before I was born, and my nanna died when I was very young. Dad was born into a fairly large family, but most of my aunts and uncles have passed away. Those who are left, and most of my cousins, I see only at weddings and funerals. It is sad but true.

During my childhood I spent a lot of time at Aunty Betty and Uncle Doug's house. My closest cousin was Ken, because he was nearest to my age. He also had an Action Man, which I never had. Several years later he married Trish, and they asked if Sue and I would sing at their wedding. I wrote a second part to Ave Maria and we sang that.

I once rode to Hartlepool to stay with Uncle Stan and Aunty Kath for a week. They were most hospitable, and Uncle Stan was very funny. Another of my aunts told Mum a story which was so funny that Mum had to bite her lip to keep from laughing. It was, all the more, funny, because my aunt was being serious, and it was so incongruous for a lady who was normally so reserved to be giving such personal details.

At one time my closest cousin was Mike. I often used to stay with Mike and Bobbie, his wife. They lived in Litchfield, so I went up by car. I photographed their son's wedding. Jamie and Alison got married at the registry office, which was covered in scaffolding, so I took some of the photos outside the cathedral.

Mike, and I, also went on a boy's week away to the Algarve. We stayed in a friend's apartment in the Vale Do Lobo. We must have been the only non-golfers there. We had a great time and two or three times we went to the King of the Toast. He would make toasted sandwiches one- foot square, with a multitude of fillings. One day, Mike asked the proprietor in fluent Portuguese, 'if you are the king, who is the queen?'

The proprietor just laughed and walked away. Once he'd gone, I whispered to Mike, 'I think you'll find he's both.'

A few years later, Mike had a small stroke. As he had subscribed to Bupa, he was in a private ward shared with only one other patient – an Irishman called Patrick. Cousin June came to visit him, and in the conversation, it came out that he was a quarter Irish. After June had left, Mike was sitting on the edge of his bed pretending to look dejected. Patrick sidled up to him and said, 'what's the matter Michael?'

Mike replied, 'you heard, I'm a quarter Irish. How much worse can it be?'

Patrick put his arm around Mike and said, as only an Irishman can, 'don't take on so Michael, at least you are three-quarters sensible.'

I have news for Mike; I have since discovered, that we are all half Irish!

At the moment, my closest cousin is June and her daughter Sue. Sue used to live near me with her husband Steve. I shall never forget one Christmas when I was playing twister with my two nephews and my dad. Steve was the twister master and kept cheating, so we were put in the most uncomfortable of positions. At one stage my face was right under my dad's bottom. I said, 'don't you even think about it.'

I was laughing so much I fell over, bringing everyone else down with me.

Sue and Steve moved to Swindon to be with June and Alan, her husband. Sadly, Steve died at only forty. The number of people at his funeral was a tribute to how popular he was. June, Alan and Sue moved to Plymouth, where I visited at least twice.

Alan also died prematurely, he was respected and liked by many of the people of Plymouth, so lots of them came to his funeral. There were also many family, colleagues and friends.

After my stroke June and Sue came to visit me at home. It was wonderful to see them, particularly because neither of them drives. I am also lucky with my extended family. I get on very well with my brother-in-law, Bob and his wife, Kim.

I love my step-kids and I am very proud of their achievements. Robert has a first- class honours degree in computer science and now works as a programmer for Intel. Tracy has a degree and a masters' in forensic psychology, and a masters' in criminal psychology. They both have wonderful partners in Esther and Dean.

Chapter 10

Motorbiking

(Song sung by Chris Spedding)

I was destined to be a biker from the age of seven. My brother Dave used to take me to school on the back of his BSA Goldstar. It was set up like a racing bike and, like most racing thoroughbreds, it was sometimes temperamental and difficult to start. On these days I had to give him a push-start.

One day, it started suddenly and left me flat on my face in the road, Dave roared around the block and picked me up on the second lap. Nothing was hurt but my pride. My school was on a very steep hill so as Dave turned into the road, he would roar up the hill, stopping outside the gates. My friends would stand by the gates waiting for me to arrive. As I got off Dave's bike, it felt good.

As soon as I was seventeen, I bought my first bike. It was a Honda 150cc and was found in someone's back garden surrounded by six-foot-tall weeds.

The battery was useless but with the aid of a car battery it started easily. I paid only ten pounds for it and it polished up beautifully. Once it had a new battery it ran well. On the way to my sister's in East Grinstead one Saturday the engine seized. Fortunately, I subscribed to a breakdown service. Within one hour the breakdown truck arrived and took the bike and me to my sister's house. My much older friend came all the way to

East Grinstead to help me remove the engine. He then took me to his workshop and showed me how to strip a bike engine. We found that it was a seized crankshaft. I found a replacement in a bike breaker's yard. We fitted the new crankshaft and rebuilt the engine. Once it was refitted in the frame the bike was in great fettle.

One day I was coming down a wet hill, it had stopped raining and the sun was out, but the road was still wet, and I was riding too fast. As I rounded a bend, I saw a car with the driver's door wide open, the driver was having a chat with a friend over the roof of the car. I must have panicked and used too much front brake, as the next thing I knew, I was flying through the air like superman. It was fun to start with, but when I hit the road, it hurt. The crash helmet saved my life, but I was rendered unconscious. Someone must have called an ambulance for I was soon in hospital. I was near home where it happened and someone must have known me, or got my address from my wallet, because when I got home the bike was there. It was surprisingly unscathed and with a new handlebar and some polish it looked good again. After the incident, I had lost faith in the bike and had to sell it.

I replaced it with a Honda 175; it was much newer and a bit bigger than the old one, but it was boring. I soon sold it and having more money than sense I bought my first new bike. It was a Yamaha RD350, it was beautiful, and it was fast. I used it to commute to work every day and the only thing wrong with the bike was that if I rode too slowly in traffic it oiled up the spark plugs and it either smoked a lot or stopped altogether. I always carried a can of goofy juice to clean the plugs.

One day I was coming home from work in the snow and I

saw another biker stranded. My knee was still hurting from the accident previously, especially in the cold weather, so I carried on going. Then I thought how mean to leave him so I went back to see if I could help. When he removed his crash helmet, he was a very attractive young lady.

As her bike was a two-stroke like mine I figured it might be the same problem. I removed the spark plug and sprayed some 'goofy juice' on it. I then replaced the plug and confidently said 'it'll restart now.' When it started, I uncrossed my fingers and breathed a sigh of relief. She asked what she could do to thank me! I said come out for a drink with me. She gave me her phone number and rode off. I thought, why did I ask her out; I am happily engaged?

I still went through with the meeting, but I invited my friend Colin along. He was a fellow biker, charming and without a girlfriend. I stayed for one drink and then made my excuses and left the two of them together. It seemed to work out because they went out for several months.

I went back to my dealer to see if they could sort out my bike's oiling up problem and they referred me to the importers, Mitsui Yamaha in Chessington. When I explained the problem, the chief mechanic took me to a test room and put my bike on a rolling road where he fixed the front wheel while the back wheel drove the rollers. The machine measured power and speed. Two gigantic vacuum cleaners extracted the fumes from the exhausts, while I rode it normally, as if I was in traffic and then I pretended I was on the motorway. When I started going fast, the extractors couldn't cope with the smoke, and it started to fill up the room. After a few minutes the chief mechanic rang in and said, 'quick get out before you die.'

They tried some experimental carburettors and they adjusted the oil flow. When I left the factory it was the fastest, cleanest running RD350 on the road.

My biking friends and I used to meet regularly to swap bike stories and chill. At one meeting, my friend, Chris came by to show off his bike, a new Yamaha XS 1100. It was a beast and it put our bikes to shame. He also said that he had started drinking at the Gun in Croydon where the Nightingales met, they were the Croydon chapter of the Hells Angels. Pandy, the leader of the Nightingales, had befriended Chris, although he made it clear that he wasn't about to join. Pandy, told him some amusing and horrific stories, like the one I'm about to tell you.

Several of the Nightingales were coming home from a party in a transit van, when a police car began to follow them. The officer noticed that the van was riding low on its rear axle so, he pulled them over. The officer was on his own, which was often the case in those days. He approached the driver and asked what he had in the back. The driver replied, 'just tools officer.

The policeman asked him to open the door of the van. He saw twelve hells angels, including Pandy, crammed in the back. The young officer looked at Pandy and asked, 'What kind of tool are you?'

Pandy replied, 'I'm a monkey wrench; wanna make something of it?'

The poor officer went pale and said, 'now, now, lads, just get home safely.'

The Nightingales drove off and, discretion being the better part of valour, the officer took no further action.

I'm now going to tell you the only other repeatable story which Chris recounted, as told to him by Pandy.

One of the Hells Angels had an accident on his motorbike which rendered it temporarily off the road. While it was being repaired, he either rode pillion on the back of someone else's bike, or, used public transport.

One day, he was standing at the bus stop when, he was attacked by a gang of Skinheads. They beat him to within an inch of his life and he ended up in intensive care. Several weeks later, having been discharged from hospital, he was standing at the same bus stop when the same gang of skinheads approached. This time there were twelve of them, however, they were unaware that behind an adjacent wall crouched six burly Hells Angels, including Pandy. Although the Skinheads outnumbered the Hells Angels by two to one, they took one look at them, turned and ran away.

I am not trying to glorify the Hells Angels, or paint them as paragons of virtue, but in those days, they appeared to be the only gang who lived by a moral code. They would never attack an innocent party and only fought with other gangs. On the contrary, the Skinheads seemed to attack indiscriminately and only fought gangs whose numbers were considerably fewer than their own.

My friend, Maf (Matthew), had a Ducati 450. I found it an interesting bike and I was longing to ride it, but I had to choose the right moment to ask. One day, Maf was chatting to an attractive young girl so I thought this was an ideal moment to ask. Maf said, in a very superior way, 'You can ride it if you can start it.'

I had seen him start it before and the technique seemed identical to my brother's BSA. It started on the first kick, much to Maf's amazement, so with a, 'cheers, Maf!'

I roared off. It wasn't as fast as my bike even though it had a bigger engine but the handling around corners was incredible.

One summer's day, we met at a pub on a main road. As it was such a nice day, we chose a table outside. We were enjoying our pints while we were watching our more adventurous friends staging a competition on the side road opposite. The aim was to ride over the hump-back bridge as fast as you could, stopping safely before the main road. Our, 'nuttiest' friend, was determined to set a record that no one else could beat. He went over the hump-back bridge at 70 mph. To begin with he looked like Eval Knievel but when he landed, he broke both rear suspension units. He then grabbed too much front brake and the bike slid on its side. Still on board the bike, he slid across the ,luckily clear, main road coming to rest under our table. He put one hand up on the table and said,

'mine's a pint!'

When I visited my brother Dave in Holland on my Yamaha, he lived in the province of Limburg which is in the south of Holland, so the most direct route is to take a ferry to Ostend and then ride across Belgium. I was on a Belgian motorway, cruising at 100 mph, when a police Porsche 911 came out of nowhere, drew alongside me and the passenger showed me his Uzi machine gun.

In those days there were no speed limits on Belgian motorways and, although I was not breaking any law, I slowed down immediately, and the police car disappeared into the distance. At the first sign to Holland, I left the motorway.

By the time I reached Dave's home I was still shaking so I told him what had happened. I forget what their real name was, but their nickname was 'The Gestapo'. Dave explained that they drove highly modified and tuned Porsche 911 turbos stripped out, so they only contained a pair of Recaro racing seats with full harness straps and a police radio. Their job was to catch drug and diamond smugglers. Their cars could outrun anything but if the smuggler was stupid enough to try to get away, they would wait for a clear piece of road and then shoot at their rear tyres. They soon stopped then. Of course, they weren't always catching smugglers so in moments of boredom they would intimidate tourists like me!

A few months after I went home, Dave came to England to visit Mum and Dad. I came over as well and Dave asked to ride my bike. He was used to bigger bikes, but he wasn't used to the power coming in that viciously, so when he took off the front wheel went up in the air. It shook him up so much he forgot which side of the road he should be on and riding on the wrong side of the road, he came face to face with a post office van. Convinced that the van was on the wrong side, he panicked and mounted the pavement. When he brought the bike back, he said he would never ride it again.

One day, my biker friends and I went to Brighton on the old Brighton road. Grot (Graham), had lost his license for a year, so he rode as pillion on one bike and his girlfriend, Clare, came on my bike. She was a great pillion and knew exactly how to lean around corners. However, she had an insatiable appetite for speed and kept thumping me on the back urging me to go faster. We came to a spiralling bend and I went into it just above the speed limit and came out of it just below the speed limit, leaving a shower of sparks from the stand behind me. There was no danger because I knew the bike very well, I had upgraded the rear suspension and had fitted the best tyres you could buy. Grot didn't see it that way, and when we reached Brighton, I was banned from taking her back.

One night, I came back from my friend's house very late. When I reached my local high street, I accelerated very hard, unaware that I was being followed by a police Rover. He only caught me because I stopped outside my parent's house. The sergeant was a very wise and honest officer. He admitted that I was accelerating so fast he couldn't read my number plate and at one stage, he lost me altogether. He added, 'but we both know you were speeding. How would it be if I were to knock on your parent's door to tell your mum that her son had died in a bike crash?'

The thought of dying had never crossed my mind, so the suggestion shook me up considerably. It, did me 'more good', than a speeding ticket would have done. I had to calm down on the bike, and the shock was exactly what I needed.

I kept the Yamaha for three years, but as I had spent a lot of money going to Italy, I could no longer afford to run it. Reluctantly I sold it and bought a little Suzuki TS90. It was a trials bike, cheap to run and fun to ride, but it was very slow. I was soon seduced by a Yamaha 125 racing bike; it was fast but very unreliable. I was on my way to visit my friend, Colin, at Southampton University when I broke down at Petersfield. I phoned the breakdown service and Colin to come to pick me up, but he broke down when he arrived. It was a fairly new bike and he had had no trouble with it before. We called it 'Petersfield triangle.'

He phoned a friend at university and he agreed to pick us both up in his car. We thought that he would break down as well, but he broke the jinx and arrived ok. Meanwhile, the breakdown lorry arrived and with a suitable bribe, he took my bike to my flat without me. Without a second thought, I returned the bike to a standard Yamaha and sold it. My finances were a lot better, so I bought a Honda CB500. When I later returned to see Colin again at Southampton University, this time I made it.

I heard that Blanchards Motorcycles were having an Italian open day, so I phoned my friends John and Phil and we went to try out their bikes. I tried 4 bikes, the first was a Moto Guzzi LeMans. This was supposed to be their sporty bike, but it was very uninteresting to ride. The second one was a Moto Guzzi Californian. It was good in a straight line but around corners it was terrible. The next bike was a Ducati Darmah, which was like riding a Japanese bike. The only impressive bike was a Ducati 900 SS. It was as if it was on rails. When you approach a roundabout, you just thought of which exit you wanted, and the bike did the rest. It was a joy to ride, let down by its instrumentation. The switches were flimsy and the speedometer broke while I was riding it. We all agreed that it was a good day out but nothing to tempt us to part with our money.

A few weeks later the three of us went to Dave Taylor's trials park, near Dartford. We each hired one of Dave's bikes as ours were not suitable and we headed for the amateur circuit. At one point the amateur and professional circuit were only separated by a flimsy tape. Someone in front of me had broken the tape so I ended up on the professional circuit, going down a very steep hill. Somehow, I reached the bottom without falling off the bike, but the rest of the circuit was very difficult and a bit scary. I was so impressed I returned my bike and never went back.

Knowing that I was going to the Isle of Mann the following year to watch the motorcycle TT, I gave my bike a full service. I found that the compression on three of the cylinders was a bit low and the fourth one was very low. I stripped the top part of the engine, reground the valves and replaced the piston rings. Once I had rebuilt the engine, I had a gentle ride to Southampton to bed in the new rings.

This time, Colin introduced me to his biker friends in Chandlers Ford. One of them owned a Kawasaki Z1. Nowadays you can buy a standard bike which will do 200 mph, but in those days the Z1 was regarded as the 'king of the road'. This particular Z1 was tuned with all Yoshimura parts and fitted with a Yoshimura exhaust. To my amazement, I was allowed to ride it around the block. It was so powerful that it was difficult to keep the front wheel on the road and it was so fast that it literally took my breath away. It was great fun to ride, but I remember thinking that if I owned such a big bike, I would never keep my licence.

As planned, three of us went to the Isle of Mann the next year. Colin had his Yamaha, 650, I had my Honda 500 and Trevor rode on the back of one of our bikes. We went for two weeks, so we could see both practice, and race meets. The practice week was organized in a way that the riders could become familiar with the course. This was difficult because one lap was 37 miles long. Also, the course was on ordinary roads and lined with buildings and stone walls.

There were many places to watch the race, but a favourite was Ballaugh Bridge. The riders would go over the humpback bridge so fast that they were airborne for several seconds. Mick Grant lived on the island and had mastered the art of landing on the front wheel. This was very dangerous, but it saved him time.

One race was called the Classic. All the riders had standard bikes. Mike Hailwood, a star of yesteryears, was riding a Ducati whilst Phil Reed was riding a Honda. On the last lap Mike was in the lead and Phil was trying so hard to catch up to him he blew the Honda up. Mike Hailwood waved to us as he rounded the corner and he went on to win the race easily.

At the end of the practice week there is a day known as 'mad Sunday' when all of the amateur riders were allowed to ride the circuit. We decided not to join them but to watch instead. No one was hurt that year, which surprised us, as they really were mad.

The next year I upgraded my bike again to a Suzuki 750 and five of us went on an extensive tour of Europe. We all had 750's but they were three very different bikes. Phil was on his Ducati with his wife, Barbara, John had a Yamaha and I was riding my Suzuki with my girlfriend, Elaine, on the back. We covered a total of 4500 miles and saw Belgium, West Germany, Austria, Yugoslavia, Greece, Corfu and Italy.

When we reached the North of Italy, we went our separate ways. Phil, Barbara and John went to Le Mans and we went to Switzerland. We went through the Grand St Bernard Pass and when we emerged in Switzerland it was twilight, so we stopped at the nearest hotel. They were very welcoming, and we had a cheese fondue which neither of us had tried before. It was made of three different cheeses, kirsch liqueur and white wine, served with crusty bread; it was delicious. In the morning we were greeted by a picturesque blue sky and a gorgeous view of Mont Blanc in the distance.

While we were in Switzerland, I wanted to see the Egli factory. Egli made their own motorcycles powered by Japanese engines. Even the engines were heavily modified and tuned. The result was a hand-built, road-legal racing bike. When we arrived at Egli we told them we were from England and were dragged into a room full of reporters. The chief mechanic was showing the latest creation on the rolling road.

Once he had demonstrated the bike's power, he took it out on the road. I took home some posters and was very happy. We went home via France where I picked up a speeding ticket along the way. The bike had gone very well but I coveted its big brother, the GS 850. It was driven by a shaft rather than a chain, so it was much cleaner. I indulged myself and bought a new one.

Elaine's parents lived in the town of Maesteg, near Bridgend in South Wales. For the rest of the summer we rode to stay with them every weekend. Where I worked at the time, we used to be a joint computer unit with the Home Office, but they were relocating to Bootle and Elaine went with them.

I changed the rear suspension of my bike, to superior units, I also bought a full fairing. My cousin, Ken, who, worked for British Airways spraying planes, offered to spray my fairing. He sprayed gold pinstripes on it as well as my monogram. The fairing made my bike run hotter, so I added an oil radiator. Soon afterwards I met Jacky and the following year we rode to the French/Italian Riviera. I went on a few, mini tours.

I went to see Dave in Holland once and I visited my mum in Devon several times. I also commuted to work every day. I liked the bike so much that I kept it for fourteen years. Even then I only sold it because I got divorced and could no longer afford to run it. The new owner was called Roger Ash, so with a small amendment, the monogram fitted perfectly. With a tear, I waved it goodbye.

I replaced it with a Kawasaki GPZ305. It was driven by a rubber belt, so it was also very clean. It was a very good commuter bike. It was very economic to ride, very reliable and very uninteresting. I soon sold it and bought its big brother the GPZ500S. It was a wonderful bike to ride but two years later I decided it was too extravagant to run as a commuter bike, so I let it go.

I then bought a Kawasaki KMX200. It was a two-stroke trials bike, and although, it was small it was great fun to ride and economic to run. Two years later it had been running badly so I booked it into a dealer in Fulham for a full service. I worked just across the river in Putney. That afternoon they phoned me to tell me that they had encountered problems and my bike would not be ready until the following day.

When I turned up to pick up my bike the next day, I was presented with an astronomical bill. I saw a beautiful second-hand bike in their showroom. It was a Yamaha FJ1200 and, although it was five years old, it had only done 2,500 miles.

When I expressed an interest in it, the manager explained that they were selling it for a customer who had bought it in his fifties, trying to recapture his youth. He hadn't realised how much bike technology had progressed since he had last ridden one. I took it for a test ride, and it was even better than it looked.

They gave me a trade-in offer, which I found perfectly acceptable, and the price of the Yamaha was very reasonable. The manager also offered to waive the service charge on the

Kawasaki. It was too good an offer to resist, so I phoned the insurance company from the office, paid the balance of the Yamaha by credit card, and rode off home. When I got back to the office and told my colleagues what I had done, they thought I was mad. I had left the office to pick up a 200cc bike and come back with one six times the size instead.

My friend Dave had just bought a mobile home near Canterbury, and he invited me to stay for the weekend. He had discovered a dual carriageway which led nowhere. The police never patrolled there, and there were no cameras. He thought it would be a good place to try out the bike.

The plan was to follow him in his Peugeot 207 and overtake at a predetermined speed. I overtook in top gear and on the homeward bound I stopped at a lay-by to let him catch up. I thought I had just cruised past him, but he said I was pulling away from him so fast that he couldn't read my number plate. I thought I would take it to the red line in the lower gears. I tried, but I couldn't cope with the acceleration. I thought the speed was impressive, but the acceleration was staggering. I thought back several years to when I rode a Z1, and it paled into insignificance.

A couple of years later I was 'outsourced', and I found myself riding into London, which was no fun at all. A year later, Liz and I bought a big Victorian house which needed a lot of restoration. It was also around the corner from a railway station which offered a very good service to London.

For reasons of finance and convenience I took the bike off the road and garaged it for, what I thought would be six months. It turned into several years. In that time several parts had perished or seized, so I started a renovation programme.

Halfway through that, I had the stroke. Our friend Alex offered to take my bike to her garage where she would store it and complete the renovation. Whether I ride it again depends on my rate of recovery, but I live in hope!

Chapter 11

Cars

I discovered cars later in life. At 24 I bought my first car which was a Ford Escort Mark I.

The registration was ELT288J so, not surprisingly, I called it Elton. Frankly, it was a bit of a wreck. With the help and guidance of my friend, Graham, I renewed both front wings and both sills. With the use of a compressor and professional spray gun I painted the whole car. I added some red pinstripes on both sides, and I had just finished polishing it, when someone scratched it all down one side. I managed to polish out the scratch and then fitted the car with russet brown Vauxhall carpets and Rover reclining seats. You had to open the doors to recline them but that was a minor inconvenience.

Sue had a similar car, but it had very poor body work, but it had a better engine than mine. Luckily Graham owned an engine hoist so with his help I swapped them over. Having suffered a cut fuel pipe and a stolen radio, I thought the car was jinxed so I sold it.

I then bought a Renault 14. It was nice to drive but was possibly the worst car I have ever bought. So much went wrong with it that I had to spend more to fix it than the car was worth. I very quickly sold the Renault and bought a Volkswagen Golf. It was very reliable and economic to run but it had a very small engine, so it wasn't very fast. After we moved, I took out a loan and bought a two- year- old Vauxhall Cavalier. It was a lovely car to drive and I kept it for many years.

My friend Hazel was selling her Polo which needed some bodywork, but overall was a good car, so I bought it. When Sue and I, sadly, went our separate ways, I offered her the Cavalier with a huge loan, or the Polo with no loan; she took the Polo

My friend Dave was selling his Mazda 626 coupé. He forgot to tell me that it had problems. I fixed all of its faults and sold it in favour of a Mazda 626 four door.

It was a lovely car and I never should have sold it, but I pined for a sportier car. I bought a Mazda 323 which was wedge shaped and had pop-up lights. It was fun to drive but one day on the way home from Herefordshire, I drove into the back of another car. I was waiting at some traffic lights behind a Chinese guy. The lights went green and we both turned right. He saw the red light which belonged to the other road, panicked and slammed on the brakes. He had ABS brakes, but I didn't and although it was a low speed impact my car went under his, causing a lot of damage. The insurance company wrote my car off.

My brother-in-law, Roger, was selling his Vauxhall Carlton. It only had one fault, but it happened on virtually every journey, making it stop entirely. It turned out to be the coil and by coincidence the new coil was faulty too. I fixed the fault, but both of us were fed up with it, so I sold it. I bought a Ford Mondeo with electric everything. This included leather seats, which were electronically adjusted and heated. It had a V6 2.6 litre engine, so it was very fast.

Liz and I were sharing the car, so it wasn't very economical to drive in town, and I also needed an estate car for my business.

Liz liked the look of the Mercedes and I was surprised by how cheaply you could buy them second hand. We saw one in Godalming and it was so nice we bought it. We kept it for several years and found that no one views it as a second- hand car; it is a Mercedes.

In 2009, I accepted early retirement from my employer, and I used some of the lump sum to buy Liz a two-year-old, very low mileage, Mercedes A150. It is a wonderful car and in a beautiful shade of metallic, ice blue. Liz has still got it and, has enjoyed driving it for over 90,000 miles. It is the long wheelbase model and, gives you a longer and wider car than the standard A class. This means more leg room and more luggage carrying capacity. In the January of 2011, my friend John gave me a lift in his Mercedes E class.

I hadn't been in it for several years, so I asked him how it was running. He said it had always run well but as it was now nine years old, he was going to buy a new one. He was shocked that the dealer was offering so little part exchange, especially as he was paying £42,000 for a new one. I said I would improve on their offer, if he would consider selling it to me. He agreed. I sold my C class very easily, as it was silver, a very popular colour. John was happy because he was now a cash buyer, with nothing to sell and had, therefore, negotiated a substantial discount. I had bought an E class for a very reasonable price. More importantly, it was once our wedding car, and was now mine.

Rather like the motorbike, whether I drive it again will depend on my recovery. In 2014, Liz bought me a mobility car, it is fitted with a winch and came with a ramp to pull me on board in my wheelchair. This has enabled me to visit home more often, and have the occasional, trip out. I have been to see the deer at Knole Park and to visit the farm, called Bore Place were Liz goes on Fridays.

I would like to end the chapter with a story about a broken-down Rolls Royce. It is supposed to be true and occurred when Rolls Royce was, an independent motor car company, and would go to great lengths to protect their reputation. It may be an apocryphal tale, but either way, it makes a good story.

A man had lost his wife prematurely to cancer. A year later he decided to indulge himself and bought a new Rolls Royce. He went on a tour of Europe and was on a Swiss mountain road when he ran over a rock which had fallen onto the road. After that, the car was still driveable, but the handling was erratic, and the back of the car was very noisy.

He hadn't subscribed to Rolls Royce breakdown cover because he thought Rolls Royce's never broke down. This, however, was an unforeseen circumstance, so he phoned his dealer in the UK. He explained what had happened and they agreed to phone him back. Moments later Rolls Royce Switzerland phoned him. When he explained his predicament, they said that a mechanic would be with him within an hour.

The mechanic duly arrived in a helicopter and when he looked at the car he diagnosed a broken half shaft. He phoned his garage and said that another helicopter would be sent to recover the vehicle by lifting it from the mountainside. The man went with the mechanic in the first helicopter and was taken to a hotel of his choice, a five-star hotel. He thought the hotel would be outside his budget but as his holiday had been curtailed, he decided to spoil himself. He ate and drank very well and enjoyed the facilities of the hotel.

Three days later his repair car was delivered to the hotel and the keys left at reception. The man then asked for his hotel bill. The receptionist said the bill had been settled by Rolls Royce. Delighted, the man drove off in disbelief and found the car was running very well, so he finished his holiday after all.

Three months later he still hadn't received a bill for the repair of the car – which indeed wasn't covered by a guarantee - so he phoned his dealer. They transferred him to Switzerland where he explained that he hadn't received a bill. He was told that Rolls Royce wouldn't be making any charge. That's what I call customer service!

Chapter 12

Love changes everything

Not counting the puppy love I felt when I was five, I first fell in love properly when I was eighteen, with Lia, an Italian girl. She was twenty- one and it was my first really emotional and passionate romance.

She was staying at the vicarage and was studying to become a teacher of foreign languages, particularly English, so she spent a good deal of her time in England. I had moved into my own flat by this time, so we were able to spend some wonderful, uninterrupted time together. She lived in Albisola Marina, next to Savona, on the Italian Riviera and I spent all my money and leave going to visit her there. She introduced me to her friends, all of whom were delightful.

One time a few of us went to a sports bar which only served exotic ice creams. The first time I went, I had one of the most popular ice creams, which was vanilla ice cream with hot espresso coffee poured over it. On the last occasion I had their most extravagant ice cream which was lemon ice cream with champagne poured over it. It was lovely. Another day, we went to a restaurant and after the meal, one of Lia's friends produced a guitar and Lia encouraged me to sing. We did a few Cat Stevens and Simon and Garfunkel songs, which seemed to go down very well.

I normally stayed in a guest house but one time I stayed with

Lia's parents. They had a big apartment which was all solid wood and marble. Papa's pride and joy was his boat. It was more of a cabin cruiser than a speedboat, but it was fairly fast. One day he took a few of us a long way out in the Mediterranean, stopping to allow us to swim. The rest of them dived in, but I had to lower myself into the water via the steps. The water was buoyant and very easy to float on my back. No one queried why I couldn't dive or swim properly, we just had a good time.

I was beginning to realise that her father was fairly wealthy, but I didn't know how rich he was until Lia sent me a postcard of Savona. When I next saw her, I showed her the postcard and jokingly asked her, 'which part of Savona does your Papa own?'

She drew a circle around a quarter of Savona and said in a serious voice, 'about that much.'

For the Italians, Easter is a bigger deal than Christmas. Once I went there at Easter time and watched the procession go by with life-sized statues. On Easter Sunday, Mama made a veritable banquet. It consisted of several courses, each accompanied by a fine wine, selected by Papa. Each wine was vintage, but my favourite was a 1964 Barolo. It was deep red, full bodied and velvety smooth. It was also fifteen percent proof, so I had to have a sleep after the meal. I probably acquired my taste for fine food and wine from Italy.

In the second year of our relationship, Lia and I got engaged. It was an unofficial engagement, signified by the exchanging of very thin, white gold rings. This is often done by students, who don't want their parents to know. Lia was willing to walk away from Papa's wealth, but not until she had obtained her doctorate.

One day her brother, Mario, was driving us on a mountain

road. He was driving very fast around a bend when he ran over a rock. Two wheels came off the road and my heart jumped into my mouth, I didn't know it was capable of beating that fast. I grabbed hold of Lia, thinking that we only had seconds to live but Mario took it all in his stride. He continued around the bend on two wheels, like something from a James Bond film, and then brought the two wheels down again.

When Lia and I were apart, we used to write regularly, but one day her letters stopped. Her best friend had just come over to England and told me that her Papa had found out about our engagement. He was furious and asked Lia why she would even consider marrying a poor English boy when she could have her pick of the rich Italians.

Lia was so pulled apart by her love for her Papa and her love for me that she had a mental breakdown. The friend said the best way I could help her was to stay away.

I thought very hard and finally decided not to go to Italy. So that was the end of a three-year relationship. I was heartbroken and it took me a long time to recover.

For over a year, I couldn't even consider dating anyone else. A friend at college invited me to a party and tried to set me up with a beautiful Spanish girl. I talked and danced with her all evening and just when she was expecting me to ask her for a date, I went home.

The following year three of us went to the Isle of Man. We were very lucky with our choice of guest house because the landlady was very friendly and her daughter, Sharon, was gorgeous. We had a bet on who could date her. To everyone's amazement including mine, I won. It turned out to be a holiday romance, as soon as we returned to England, it was at an end.

I was working in Dunstable for a week, helping a supplier to design some software. One evening, I went into a local pub for a drink and noticed a young girl sitting at the bar looking very sad. I bought her another drink and started talking to her. It transpired that she was waiting for someone who didn't turn up. Eventually, we went to her parent's house for coffee and we started seeing each other.

One fine weekend I invited Nikki down to London to have a ride on my friend's boat. I didn't mention that my friend was a police sergeant and his boat was a police launch, powered by two turbo-charged engines. We cruised up and down the Thames for the afternoon with Nikki sitting on the back seat, enjoying the sunshine and trailing her hand in the water. When we were returning, we saw the police in action as they saved a potential suicide at Waterloo Bridge. After they had got her on board, she explained that her boyfriend had just dumped her, and she was considering jumping into the Thames.

They were very compassionate and took her back to the station for a cup of tea and a chat. A few weeks later, Nikki and I separated because of the geographical distance between us.

I first met my next girlfriend, Heather, in a self-service restaurant in Bromley. She was serving behind the till and before I left, I asked her for a date. She said yes and we were seeing each other for a few months. She was South African and attractive, but with a fiery temper. One day I dared to ask if she agreed with apartheid. She answered, 'oh no, man, I think everyone should be treated equally.'

Encouraged by this reply, I added, 'so you wouldn't mind going for a drink with a black man?'

'Oh no, man, I wouldn't want to socialise with them,' she

replied. It was obvious that her prejudice was ingrained.

She announced that she was going on a working holiday in Europe for three months. We agreed to meet in Paris at a certain time and place. When we met, we argued for twenty-four hours. It was obvious that the holiday wasn't going to work out for us as a couple, so I dumped my spare helmet in a bin and rode off.

I met Sue in a show. She was playing Rosalinda, the lead, in *Die Fledermaus* and I was in the chorus. We became friends, and that was as far as I was prepared to take it as, she was a married woman with two kids. I didn't realise that her husband was a wife beater. He would go to the pub every Friday night and would come home drunk, taking his aggression out on Sue.

Late one night, she arrived at my flat saying that he had been particularly violent, and she had nowhere else to go. I saw his car outside, so he had obviously followed her. He must have been drunk in charge and slept the night in his car. I offered Sue my room and said that I would sleep on the sofa. She refused and slept on the sofa herself. The next morning, the doorbell rang very early. I knew it was him and, as I descended the stairs, I was nervous to the point of shaking. I prayed that I might have the strength to greet him and as I reached the front door my shakes subsided.

I opened the door, and, to my surprise, I said, 'you've got a nerve coming around here after what you've done.'

He was shocked and completely disarmed. Then I said something which seems bizarre now but seemed right at the time, 'I suppose you had better come in for a cup of tea.'

He was surprised to find Sue sleeping on the sofa and, only when she agreed, I left them alone for five minutes while I made the tea. When I returned, I said it was up to her whether she went back to the family home or not. She didn't, but she went to stay with her friend. After her divorce, our relationship flourished, and we were married a few years later.

After our marriage, we lived in my flat in Hither Green, and her daughter, Elaine, joined us. It was a difficult relationship initially, as I wasn't old enough to be a father figure to Elaine, and I wasn't young enough to relate to her either.

Sue and I had some good times, including one night when we went to our local pub. We came back having had one or two drinks too many and reached home before we realised that neither of us had a key. We borrowed next door's ladder and tried to shunt it around the corner of the building. In doing so Sue fell in the pond. When I finished laughing, I helped her out and positioned the ladder by the second floor, bath-room window. I climbed the ladder, removed the louvres, and climbed in through the window. I nearly landed head-first in the toilet but somehow, I landed in a heap on the floor. I found my keys, then ran down the stairs to open the door for Sue.

We also had some good holidays. We went on a cruise up the Thames with our friends Barbara and Keith. We went to the Lake District, and to see my mum in Devon several times. We also went to Malta, Lake Maggiore in Italy and to my friends' villa in Ibiza.

One time, we were coming back from Earl's Court during the tube strike. There were very few trains and the queues from the opposite platforms were standing back to back with our platform. Suddenly a short man came pushing through the crowd. He elbowed me in the ribs and then he elbowed Sue. I grabbed him by the lapels and pulled him up on his toes until we were nose to nose. Then I said, "you can elbow me, but you don't touch my wife."

He spat some obscenities at me in a strong, Glaswegian accent. I said "Just shut up. There is a train coming, do you want to be in it or under it?"

He spat some more obscenities at me, wriggled free and ran up the stairs heading for the exit. Sue flung her arms around me and exclaimed 'my hero.'

My adrenalin had drained quickly, and I completely went to pieces.

When we moved to Chislehurst, we became estranged, as we were leading separate lives. It was, partly, the fault of our involvement in various operatic productions. We were both doing lots of shows, and usually different ones. Three years later, against my beliefs and principles, we got divorced. It was a mutual decision and as far as possible an amicable divorce. It must have been fairly amicable, because a couple of years later, Sue asked me to make Elaine a wedding cake. Nine years after our divorce, she came to the church when I got remarried to Liz. She has also visited me in hospital several times since my stroke.

Sometime later, I was in a production of *Into the Woods*, when I met Kim. It was a mere coincidence that Kim went to the same school as Elaine, but it was far more embarrassing to learn that Kim was in the year below Elaine.

We were dating for several years, and we shared some nice holidays. We went to Ibiza, Venice, Lake Como and Turkey. In Turkey we met a man called Hassan. He owned a boat and his main business was to carry up to twenty tourists between resorts. You could, however, charter him for the day.

We met another English couple and we all went out in Hassan's boat, costing us only fifty-five pounds per couple. This included some superb food, as he used to be a chef in Istanbul. He also had a huge chest full of iced water and drinks, alcoholic and non-alcoholic, all of which were free.

We enjoyed the day so much that we went back on our own, this time it cost us seventy pounds. We went right out to sea and, discovering a cove with only one boat in it, he said it was too busy. We found an empty cove and he lent me his snorkel, face mask and flippers. The colourful fish and coral were fascinating.

A few days later, we went to Turtle Beach on a remote Island. We saw no turtles and the boat left early, without us, so we had to pay double to get back in another boat. Later we saw our friend Hassan drinking at a bar, and he asked us how the day was. We told him what had happened and the next thing we knew the captain was frogmarched in front of us. He was made to kneel down, apologise and give us a full refund.

The next day, I booked a ride on a jet bike. When we returned someone had crashed the bike, so I was asked to come back in half an hour. When I came back, I was lent the owner's bike. It was a lot faster than the others, so I was asked to stay in sight. It was so fast that the next thing I knew, I had passed three bays. When I came back, I apologised and returned the bike intact.

We also went on a mini cruise from Turkey to Egypt to see the Pyramids at Cairo. When we arrived, we were ushered into one of the Pyramids.

There was nothing to see, but the experience was surreal. Once outside, I took copious photographs of the pyramids and the Sphinx. Then I pointed my camera at a guard on a camel.

He was obviously camera-shy because he aimed his machine gun at me in return. I lowered my camera, raised my hands and apologised. The guard lowered his weapon and relaxed, so I walked away, quickly, feeling content as I had managed to get the photo.

When we returned to Turkey, we bumped into our friend, Hassan, and invited him for a drink. He didn't need to reciprocate, but he invited us to his friend's restaurant on our last night.

Meanwhile I had learnt to barter. I haggled for ages over a marble chess set. When we had agreed on a reasonable price, it was all smiles, but when he was cleaning the pieces, a head broke off one of the knights. He was most apologetic because it was the last of that type. Not wishing to make a fuss, I bought a simpler chess set for a reduced price.

On our last night, we met Hassan at his friend's restaurant. We were seated at a large table with several of Hassan's friends and we had a lovely meal. Then we noticed that his friends were getting up one by one and leaving without paying. We thought that it was an elaborate sting, being the last to leave, and left with an enormous bill! We were thinking like Westerners because Hassan paid the whole bill. The next day we returned to England and promised we would come back.

On the day of my mum's funeral, Kim and I drove to Potters holiday camp in Norfolk, which was her family's favourite place. It was not good timing, because my mother had just died. Also, I do not like holiday camps and this one was very sport-orientated, which I like even less.

Seven years after we met, and without any reason or warning, she ended the relationship. There was no one else involved;

she was just becoming a career girl. It took me even longer to come to terms with the situation than did my divorce, probably because it was so sudden, and Kim gave me no reason for her decision.

Eighteen months after we split up, I was performing in *The Beggar's Opera* at the Beckenham Theatre Centre and I met Liz, who was working front of house. We both thought that the meeting was by chance, but it was engineered by two friends, Fiona and Eunice. So, while John Drewery was doing a splendid job of directing The Beggars Opera, his wife Eunice was doing a great job of directing us! I don't usually approve of arranged meetings but, in this case, we owe a debt of gratitude to them because without their intervention we may have never met.

Sadly, both of my parents had passed away, as had Liz's father, but we visited her mother fairly often, she lived in Kington, Herefordshire, and was married to Derek.

About a year after we met, Liz was window-shopping in West Wickham and saw a ring, which she fell in love with. She came back and told me about it and I knew I was ready for commitment, so I secretly went to the jewellers and bought it.

We were going to stay with her friends in Rome in three months' time, so I kept the ring hidden. When Liz saw the ring had gone, she was very upset and said to me,

'My ring has gone'.

I said,

'It was never yours to start with.'

To keep the subterfuge going. I am normally not very good at keeping my own secrets, but I am, also an incurable romantic; the romantic won.

When we arrived in Rome it was glorious weather so, after Liz had introduced me to her friend, Alexandra, I suggested that the two of us go into the centre. Alexandra's daughter, Letizia showed us onto the right bus and came part of the way with us. When we reached the centre, I said that it might be nice to see the Trevi Fountain in the sunshine; I sat Liz down on the edge of the fountain.

Then, I went down on one knee and proposed in Italian, producing the ring she had seen three months before. She said yes, but she probably thought I was asking if she wanted an ice cream!

They say you can get lost in a crowd, which is quite true. No one saw us except one lady up at street level, who asked me what Liz had said. I told her Liz had said, 'No.'

Then I said that I was joking, and she had actually said, 'Yes.'

The lady then shouted,'Bravo!' And she continued to clap and shout,'Bravo!'

An opportunist flower seller came rushing over and, although I knew I was being ripped off, I could hardly refuse. I bought Liz some red roses and we headed back to the apartment, after throwing some coins in the fountain.

When we arrived, Alexandra introduced me to her husband Luciano, who had just returned from work. When I gave them our good news, Luciano produced a bottle of champagne, which he happened to have chilling in the fridge. Later that week, we went to one of their favourite restaurants to celebrate further.

We didn't think we could be married in church as we were both divorced and our church was in an interregnum period, between vicars. We made our case to Penny Avann, the local

Canon, and Nick Reid, our Deacon. Soon after that, Nick Lang was appointed vicar, so we had to plead our case again, but this time it was with the recommendation from Penny and Nick.

We had been going to St John's, Eden Park, for some time, so I told Nick that, although we would love to be married in church, we would rather have a blessing at St John's, than tout around until we found a church. Eventually, Nick agreed to marry us, and even allowed us to use the venue free of charge.

The day itself, was unforgettable. Although we were on a tight budget, we compromised on nothing, except numbers. With around fifty people seated and another seventy arriving in the evening. For the service, Liz wore a beautiful ivory wedding dress with coffee and peach embroidery on the bodice. I wore a pale gold brocade frock coat. Liz was given away by her son, Rob and her bridesmaid was her daughter, Tracy. My best friend Mark was my best man. Our friends did everything they could to make the day special. John offered to be our chauffeur in his new E. class Mercedes. Iona, John's wife, assembled a group comprising James, Katie, Martin and Ronnie to sing for us during the signing of the register. Mike Spencer, my old choir master, played the organ, the church was free of charge and Pat Freeman gave us the flowers as a wedding present.

After the service we built in an hour of our day to share a glass of wine with those friends who came to the church but weren't coming to the reception.

We had hired the hall and Jeff and Julia had agreed to serve refreshments. The weather was so beautiful when we came out of the church, that they had erected a gazebo and were serving the wine outside. For our reception we had a carvery and Sharpie, the head chef, had explained that we could have three of the four joints of meat. We had chosen lamb, beef and turkey, but Liz had said it was a pity because she loved pork. To our surprise, on the day Sharpie had added pork and crackling just for the top table!

We had the Bow Belles, a female string quartet, serenading us throughout the meal. Mark gave a wonderful speech during which, he produced a rude apron which I thought I had lost on the stag do. He also said, 'I have known Paul for fifteen years and we've never had a cross word, although there was that time when I didn't speak to him for 3 months. I didn't like to interrupt!'

Everyone laughed and I really don't know why!

One of our friends, Robert Hedden, generously offered us his villa in Ibiza for our honeymoon, which, at peak- season would, usually, have cost a thousand pounds. Mark had the keys and said he would only hand them over if I sang. I said I would but only if James joined me in a duet. We sang Bizet's *The Pearl Fishers Duet* from the opera *The Pearl Fishers*. We did a passable job, considering we had no accompaniment.

In the evening we had a buffet, free bar and a Ceilidh band who played mainly traditional Irish music, and included a few 'Corrs' tracks.

I have already said that we spent our honeymoon in Robert's villa, but Liz's kids had given us a bottle of Dom Perignon to take with us. We enjoyed it on the terrace.

Liz's mum couldn't come to the wedding because she had suffered a stroke. We went up to Kington to visit her.

In the years after the wedding, Liz and I enjoyed some lovely holidays, including: Kephalonia, Costa del Sol, The Algarve, Scotland, Goa and Tenerife. Liz has always said that she hopes we will celebrate our Golden Wedding anniversary. We will both be old, but I guess we can make it.

Chapter 13

Wherever I lay my hat that's my home
(Song by Paul Young)

I was born in Mayday Maternity Hospital in Croydon, on Friday 13 January 1956. That probably doesn't count because I didn't wear a hat and it wasn't my home. I spent the first four years of my life in a council 'pre-fab'. Although it was well past its sell-by date, they tell me it was very nice. My Mum and Dad certainly hosted a lot of family parties there.

When I was four, we were relocated to a terraced house in Elmers End. My parents didn't much like it there, so they moved back to South Norwood. Our next door but one neighbours in Elmers End were the Peacocks' and when we moved, they were our next door but one neighbour again. This time it was an end of terrace house and the terrace consisted of only three houses.

I was lucky, before I left home, because I was in the Peacocks' house when their friend Don came to visit. He managed several flats in the neighbourhood and one happened to be vacant. It was a ground floor studio flat in a very big Victorian house. It had it's own kitchen and bathroom, but shared a toilet with one other flat. I was very happy there until I met the man upstairs. The fact that he was gay didn't bother me. The fact he turned out to be a pervert did. I heard that Miss Andrews, an elderly lady from our church, had a flat to let, so I moved to Upper Norwood.

The flat consisted of a spacious lounge, a kitchen/diner and a large bedroom. I had my own toilet but had to share a bathroom, which was my excuse for being late for work. Miss Andrews charged me a very modest rent and she wasn't very rich, so I felt it was my responsibility to fix problems as they arose. This included the time I was looking out of the lounge window and the bottom of the lower sash fell out. I pulled my head inside before the glass fell out. It saved me from potential decapitation. The sash was rotten, so I rebuilt it and had it re-glazed. A couple of years after I moved in, the kitchen units fell apart and the sink looked fairly insanitary. I built new units and I fitted a, stainless steel, sink. I also made an L-shaped unit on the opposite wall.

I stayed with Miss Andrews for seven years and then I bought my first home. It was a three bedroomed maisonette, converted from a semi-detached Victorian house.

The feeling of putting the key in the lock and setting foot across the threshold was indescribable. I stood in the middle of an empty lounge arms outstretched and spun around thinking 'this is all mine'. I would have shouted it, but my friends were not far behind. I rebuilt the kitchen but kept the oven, which was built in and had a rotisserie. because it worked well.

The only access, into the loft, was a trapdoor above the bath. This wasn't very convenient, so I climbed into the loft with a torch, crawled forward and made a new hole above the land-ing. I made a hatch, fitted a loft ladder and boarded the loft. I then fitted a Velux window, ran power and light to the loft and turned it into a workshop. While I was working in the loft, my dad lent me a circular saw. He failed to mention that to make it fit the bench, he had taped the power switch permanently on and had removed the blade safety guard. As soon as I plugged it in, it whirred into life and nearly cut my leg off.

Sue and I hosted several after show parties. The flat was ideal for this, with its large rooms, three split levels and two bathrooms. I persuaded my friend who was a qualified electrician to rewire the whole lighting system. I wanted to be able to switch on and off the three landing lights from the main landing. At one point, Lee,the electrician, was standing on the main landing with a fist full of cables. I asked him how he knew what each cable did. He said that he had notched the sheath of each cable in an ingenious code. I must have been distracting him because while I was talking, he stripped all the sheaths off. I looked at the floor and asked, 'where are your codes now?'

I won't repeat what he said, but it's not in the Oxford English Dictionary. We had to test all of the cables to see where the other end was.

My neighbours, in the flat downstairs, found an injured fox that they nursed back to health. They then decided to keep it, and Barry made a cage out of wood and chicken wire. They soon tired of it and stopped cleaning the cage on a regular basis. The stench was unbelievable, and I could never open my kitchen window. The public health department was not interested because it was being kept as a pet. The RSPCA were not interested because it was vermin.

When my neighbours had their first baby, they wanted to get rid of the fox but were faced with a dilemma. If they let the fox go it might be too domesticated and not survive. My friend Godfrey arrived in his land rover with attached trailer. He posed as an animal lover who lived in a big house with acres of land. He was a thespian friend, and this was his finest role. Once he had appeased their conscience, they gave him the fox. He drove straight to some common land and released it.

When we tried to sell the flat, we found it was blighted by the Channel Tunnel Link. They were proposing to go underground at Hither Green. Although none of the proposed plans were within half a mile of my house, the whole of Hither Green was rendered unsaleable. In 1990, it was announced that the Eurostar would run above ground using existing rail tracks. Suddenly our flat was saleable. Despite the housing recession, we received an offer for nearly three times the amount I had paid for it, only 7 years before. In addition, our buyers had no chain behind them. We were so anxious not to lose them we offered them vacant possession and moved in with Sue's mother, Eileen Norton. She was most hospitable, but they were a very long 10 weeks.

We stored all of our furniture, and 50 boxes containing all of our possessions, in a friend's double garage. It was filled to the ceiling. I bought a new padlock for the garage door and we visited every Saturday morning. One week, the door had been forced open and everything had gone. The police likened it to a fire, because we lost everything. The newspapers were very good to us, one paper published a front-page article with a photo, appealing to the thieves to return anything that they didn't want. Nothing was returned. The insurance company paid for all the tangible things such as furniture and electrical items. However, the items of enormous sentimental value to us, and no value to anyone else, were lost forever.

Once we had 'completed' we returned to the market in a very strong position. In Chislehurst, we found a three bedroomed, semi-detached house, with garage, at a very reasonable price. The previous owner was an architect and he had designed and built a very large extension. This gave us a twenty-one foot long, by seventeen foot wide, lounge and a very large kitchen, behind the garage. There was very little to do to the house, but I did fit a loft ladder and a Velux window. Also, the windowsill to the bow window, was very thin and had been curled by the sun. I designed and had made, a thicker one, which I subsequently fitted.

We continued to host after show parties, until a member of the cast, foolishly, invited a few people from the band. They arrived empty handed and attacked the food like they hadn't eaten for weeks. They also drank anything they could lay their hands on. Initially, I thought it was quite funny. One of them put Sue's furry Gremlin on top of the ceiling fan and turned it on. Gizmo flew off the fan and dived headfirst into the trifle! Things then deteriorated rapidly, and they started throwing food at each other. One of the band members, then put my armchair into a 'recline' position, while a young girl was sitting in it drinking red wine. The wine spilt all over her clothes and my light grey armchair. He then said that white wine would remove the red wine stain. He took the girl outside and poured a bottle of white wine over her. She was soaked as well as hysterical. Sue found her a change of clothes, and the chairs removable cover, was easily cleaned. However, I felt it was time to end the party. Sue and I couldn't face the mess that night, so we left it until morning. We both regretted leaving it as it looked worse in the daylight. Food was trodden into the carpet and stuck on the walls. It was a mess.

One day I noticed a leak from the cast iron guttering at the side of the building. I climbed on to the flat roof of the kitchen. I then, rather stupidly, put a stepladder on to the corrugated roof of the garage, with a board to spread the load. I climbed the ladder to see if I could do anything to repair the gutter. Unfortunately, it was so rusty that a four- metre length of guttering came away in my hand. It was heavy. With the benefit of hindsight, I should have dropped it, but I had a split second to think. Instead of falling off the ladder I stepped off and crashed through the garage roof on the way down I hit another ladder and was thrown onto my side. If I had landed squarely on my feet, I would have broken both my legs, if not killed myself.

My neighbour, Jacquie, must have heard my yell from across the road because she came running over to see if she could help. One leg was swollen up like an elephant, so Sue phoned for an ambulance. The ambulance came quickly and took me to hospital. Miraculously nothing was broken. The lovely Irish nurse attending me said that I must have had a guardian angel. I said that if I had one, I would rather have been left on the ladder.

Sue and I only lived in the house for three years before we parted. I took on a bigger mortgage and came close to negative equity, but I kept the house. I lived in it for another eight years and then, as I was engaged to Liz, I sold it.

Liz also sold her town house in West Wickham, and we bought a three-storey Victorian house in Beckenham. It was a lovely house but needed lots of work. Our friend Paul the electrician rewired the entire house. This was a big job because the house comprised twelve rooms, a loft and a cellar. We also got our friend James to install central heating which was also a big job as it involved fourteen radiators.

I converted one of the bedrooms into an office and laid oak floor. Liz had the room next door as a craft room and it only needed a carpet and a new window. The small bedroom had been converted into a dark room. I bought a Durst enlarger from my friend Mark and I had changed my camera to a digital one before I could use it. I had the dark room changed into a shower room. I laid another oak floor to the biggest bedroom and bought a set of oak furniture.

The bathroom was so bad that one of our more outspoken friends said, 'if my bathroom was like that, I'd give up washing.'

We got tradesmen in and transformed it. We bought a large Jacuzzi bath, a large shower cubicle with a power shower and a marble topped vanity unit.

We scraped all the wallpaper off the stairwell walls. David, our friend and builder re-plastered the walls as necessary. Adrian then lined the walls and painted them. Steve then carpeted two main landings, two minor landings and all the stairs.

The ground floor boasted of its original features, including a tiled floor in the hall, stained glass windows, two fireplaces and ornate coving and roses. The lounge needed a lot of work, some of which I did, and some was carried out by tradesmen. I bought a mini scaffold platform and started stripping the coving. You would expect there to be several layers of paint after a hundred- and- twenty years, but someone had finished it in gloss paint. I stripped it back with 'Peelaway', which is highly caustic and meant for the trade. I therefore wore overalls long rubber gloves and I bought a gas mask. I must have looked like something from Star Wars! I let the Peelaway do its work and then finished the job with plastic tools and a small brush. I worked on the coving in 2ft sections and when a wall was finished, I neutralised the 'Peelaway' with white vinegar and then washed it with water. When the whole job was finished, I painted it with emulsion.

The whole job took a year of my spare time, but the end result was worth it, I had the bay window replaced with craftsmen built double glazed sashes. David, then re-plastered where Paul, the electrician had provided the wiring for wall lights, Adrian then lined the walls and I painted them. We then bought matching wall and ceiling lights. Steve fitted a carpet and we had curtains made to measure.

For our comfort, we bought a modern leather three-piece suite. We had a Victorian replica wall unit made in hard wood and found a beautifully restored, chaise longue. I polished the marble fire surround and had a flame effect gas fire installed. I had the gas pipe hidden under the floor in the cellar and I added a brass rail around the hearth and a companion set of brass fire tools to give the illusion of a real fire. We then completed the room by adding two large Victorian photographic portraits of my ancestors, two Victorian pictures given to us by Iona and a Victorian drawing of the Trevi Fountain in Rome where we got engaged.

Next door, in the dining room, the coving had already been restored, so we had it decorated professionally, to an Asian theme. I added a ceiling fan and a large mirror. Liz added her collection of two hundred and fifty elephants, and a selection of hats. Her dining room furniture was big and chunky and made in Pakistan. We finished the room with Liz's photographs of the Taj Mahal.

The kitchen was very old and tired too, so we threw it away and started again. Although we wanted modern, we also wanted to pay lip service to the Victorian age themes. We chose units that had light oak doors and draw fronts and we had the chimney breast opened to see how big it was. It was big enough for an 1100mm wide cooker, so we bought a range master.

We fitted the utility room with white units, a washing machine, a fridge/freezer and a chest freezer. I had the two windows replaced with double glazed units and we had a new back door. The downstairs cloakroom needed a new window, toilet and washbasin. Apart from that, it was perfect.

I insulated the cellar including the crawl space under the kitchen which was unlit. I put a working light attached to an extension lead the other end of which I gave to Liz to plug into a socket. I went back into the crawl space in the dark and when the light came on, I realised that my face was just inches away from the rotting corpses of a squirrel and a pigeon. I came out of the crawl space very quickly and when I had composed myself, I went back under to remove the bodies.

At the front of the house we had a wonderful veranda style porch made in wood. Unfortunately, much of it was rotten. I commissioned a joiner to make new components and David fitted them. The five stone steps were loose, so I got Adrian to help me repair them.

The side gate was also rotten, so I rebuilt it. The side alley was just mud, so I had it paved. I did a lot to the garden. When we bought the house, it was very mundane and all grass. I built a new low fence and gate across the garden to separate off the vegetable patch. I built a green house, four raised beds and a gazebo. Together we dug a pond and we used the surplus earth to make a rockery. I built a retaining wall in breeze block, and then I hid the breeze blocks with limestone rocks. The rocks were my first buy on eBay. Two ton of limestone rocks from a farm in Derbyshire.

When I had won the bid, I phoned the owner to arrange delivery. When I gave my address, he couldn't believe his ears. He was brought up just around the corner and his best friend had sold us the house. Because of the incredible coincidence, he offered to deliver the rocks himself. When he arrived, we showed him the house. He seemed to approve of what we had done, as we had kept the character of the house. We had just made it more comfortable. He couldn't stay for dinner, but he had tea and cake.

He showed me how to build a dry stone wall and then he left.

The last thing I did, was to have the conservatory rebuilt. The old one was small and rotten, so I designed one twice the size. I helped David to cast the foundations and then I employed Dave Wall to build a cavity wall. The inner skin was breeze block and the outer skin was reclaimed bricks. I also ordered a bespoke cast iron staircase and the conservatory was built on top of the wall. The conservatory was finished, and the floor was started after I had my stroke, so I never set foot in it.

Several months later, I visited home and six people had to carry me in my chair up five stone steps just to reach the front door. It wasn't a very elegant entry. Once in the house, it was obvious I could only access two rooms. I came home once more, but could only access the garden. Liz did the only thing she could and sold the house in favour of a bungalow.

I know you have to let go of a house when you sell it, but I was in hospital when it was sold. So, part of me still lives there.

Liz organised a very impressive loft extension to the bungalow, to create accommodation for a 'carer'. So, we are now the proud owners of a large, 5 bedroomed, detached, chalet bungalow, with a garage.

Chapter 14

Fitness first

In my late teens, and the whole of my twenties, it seemed like I could eat and drink anything I wanted without gaining an ounce. Several people said that would all change when I was thirty. They were wrong, because I reached thirty and nothing changed. Thirty-one was a different matter altogether, because I started piling on the pounds. I guess three things had changed in my life; no doubt my metabolism had slowed down, but I was also doing a fairly sedentary job and very little exercise.

When I lived with my parents, I used to jog around Norwood Lakes in the early morning. If the gate was still locked, I would climb over the fence. When I moved to Upper Norwood, I used to jog around Crystal Palace track, and I joined the Crystal Palace karate club for fitness rather than self-defence. When I started working at Highbury Corner, I joined the Sobell Centre at Holloway to do their circuit training twice a week. The course was run by an ex-US marine and consisted of a gruelling two- hour session, culminating in a five- mile run, (yes, I mean run). I also used to play squash and tennis.

By the time I was in my late twenties, my main activity was performing in musicals. The only exercise I had was when they gave me a part which involved dancing such as in the musicals: The Boyfriend, Godspell, Oklahoma or Kiss me Kate. Godspell was particularly energetic, and in a two-week run, I had to have my costume adjusted twice. In latter days, my only exercise had been walking the dog or walking to the pub! However, going to the pub does involve a lot of exercise, lifting a pint glass or throwing a dart. I have never been seriously, overweight, but it was probably time to lose a few pounds.

At some point in my thirties, I bought a set a of golf clubs sand started to play. I had played before but not since school when I played with my friends as an alternative to any other form of sport, I have already said that I am not very good at team sport such as football and cricket, so this seemed a good alternative.

Golf is not a particular energetic sport but, it is very good exercise as you walk for miles before you complete the course. In my case, I walk extra miles looking for my ball.

In my twenties I also took up squash. I enjoyed this but soon found myself with no partner because my main partner had moved.

I also started to play tennis, which I enjoyed very much. I haven't played for a long time, but I still maintain a keen interest.

Chapter 15

Am I defined by what I do?

I've have been a housing engineer, a structural engineer, a surveyor, a computer programmer, a computer operator, an installation planner, a systems analyst, a test manager, a project manager, a photographer, a singer and an actor.

My first part-time job was when I was thirteen and I became a paper boy. I did my round before school every morning. I gave up that job later and became a milkman's assistant. I'm afraid his name was Joe not Ernie and his milk float was battery-driven not horse-drawn. When I was old enough, I started a Saturday job at Tesco. I didn't like the manager so, I left and went to Davy Gregg, who paid about the same money but treated me much better. I served behind the cold meat and cheese counter, selling the products by either weight or number of slices.

I left school and joined the Greater London Council (GLC) at seventeen. I was a trainee civil engineer and was sponsored by the GLC to go to college one day a week to do an ONC and HNC in civil engineering. During my first year I worked in the housing engineer's office, who sometimes took in work from other councils. My main job was working on an architect's drawing of the Croxted Road Estate in Thetford.

One day my boss was sick, and I had to represent him at a meeting in Thetford. I was very nervous so the night before

I couldn't sleep, which made matters worse. On the train, I felt good for nothing, so I tried some transcendental meditation. When I arrived, I felt wide awake and I found myself controlling the meeting. I wish I could feel that way every day. I know I should have kept practising this form of meditation but at the age of eighteen, I was more interested in girls. If I had my otherwise OK career might have been outstanding.

During my second year, I worked in the structural engineer's office. I'm sure I learnt something there, but I can't remember what. In the third year, I worked for the city district surveyor's office. The most memorable day was when my boss took me to inspect the pile foundations of the Nat West Tower. I watched him being lowered down the pile hole in a cage wearing a miner's helmet; I was happy to remain on terra firma.

At the end of the third year I was asked which office I preferred. I chose the district surveyor's office, I went to Shoreditch. I went out with my boss and we were inspecting one site when we noticed a wall which the bricklayer had just built. It was neither straight nor vertical, so my boss told the bricklayer to knock it down and rebuild it. The bricklayer was so annoyed he said, 'if you're so clever, you can build it yourself.'

My boss took off his jacket, rolled up his sleeves and borrowed an overall. He kicked down the wall and laid five courses of brick quickly and efficiently. I was amazed, and the bricklayer was astonished.

One of my colleagues had resigned, so we all made sure we had no appointments that Friday afternoon. We took him over the road to a pub. Everyone was there except the District Surveyor (DS), who was conspicuous by his absence. When we returned, George went into the gents and found himself standing at the urinal next to the DS. The DS said, 'I hear you are leaving today, George. Sorry, I didn't come to the pub, I don't do that sort of thing.'

Then he turned to George and without washing his hands, he shook George's hand and said, 'good luck George.'

He later said it was the nearest he had ever come to receiving a golden handshake from the boss.

Unfortunately, the GLC didn't pay me enough to support my regular trips to Italy, so I started another job. Every evening I made fibre glass motorbike chain cases for Peter Furlong. I also had a Saturday job running an electronic shop.

I worked in Shoreditch for a year and then moved to the Highbury & Islington district surveyor's office, based at Highbury Corner. I preferred it there because I was more experienced and was given my own patch. Most of my jobs were straight forward as I would never interfere with a good builder who knew the bylaws and followed them. There was however, a four storey Victorian house, the work for which, I had to stop. I found a labourer in the basement merrily knocking down a load bearing wall with a sledgehammer. I asked him where the RSJ was. He said it would come the following day. I told him to stop working until he got some support under the floors above.

On a very dismal day, I found myself on a scaffolding of another three-storey Victorian house. I was at the roof level and there was no guard rail, so the only thing between me and a 30ft drop was hope. Fortunately, I had no fear of heights then. I produced my yard stick, which enabled me to reach the tiles I couldn't otherwise reach. The builder had apparently used no nails. except the bottom row, and even those were not galvanised. I told him to strip the roof and do it properly. He stopped his work and said, 'you and I both know it isn't properly nailed but they are concrete interlocking tiles and we would both be long gone before the roof blew off. So, you would be a hard man to insist that I do the roof again.'

He took a step towards me and said, 'have you noticed how bad the weather is? No one is out walking, so no one would hear the scream.'

I suddenly got very scared and said, 'I see what you mean. In that case....' I stepped back until I had one foot on the ladder, and then I said, 'You'll have to do the roof again.'

I raced down the first ladder and transferred to the second ladder. As I descended it, I saw a labourer waiting for me with a shovel. I swung to the underside of the ladder, dodged the labourer and ran for my bike. I roared up the road, stopping to put on my crash helmet, once I was out of harm's way.

When I reached the office, I must have looked as white as a ghost and I was still shaking. My boss wasn't there, so Bob asked what the problem was. I told him the story and he said he would go to the site immediately. He was big enough to handle himself, but he took Doug along for good measure. He would have never told me what happened, but Doug did. When they arrived at the site Bob recognised the culprit from my description. He was still on the scaffolding, so Bob called him down, then slammed him against the wall, slid him up the wall until his feet left the ground, and said, 'don't ever intimidate one of my colleagues again.'

Bob then told the builder to fix a guard rail to the top level of scaffolding and he ordered him to strip the roof tiles and nail them properly. When they returned to the office, Bob told me not to return to the site because he was taking over. I was very relieved and thanked him for his intervention.

I was missing my fiancé, Lia, very much because I hadn't seen her for three months. She told me she was flying to England on a working day and I couldn't get any time off, so I arranged to meet her at a park near a station in Highbury, at midday. I managed to go to all my visits in two hours and met her as arranged. It was such a nice day that we just lay on the grass and talked for hours. I returned to the office at the normal time and was called in to see Mr Thomas, one of the deputy district surveyors. He asked me how I was getting on, and if I had managed all my visits today. He was particularly interested in the afternoon. I spun him a suitable story and he seemed satisfied, but that night I couldn't stop thinking about the way I had lied to Mr Thomas and, I resolved to tell him the whole truth.

The next day I walked into Mr Thomas' office and I told him the whole story. He thanked me for my honesty and said he already knew half the story because he had received a telephone call from a foreman who didn't think I had given his site my fullest attention. Mr Thomas had then phoned several of my other sites and he hadn't found any that I had visited that afternoon. He further said, if I had confided in him earlier, he would have given me the time off and I wouldn't have had to work that day. It was a valuable life lesson and one I have followed to this day, never lie.

One of my sites belonged to the council. It was a fairly large plot and the council were having several low-rise flats built. The foreman must have had a lot of patience for in the early days whenever I was inspecting reinforcements, I would measure each bar and spacing. However, with experience I was soon able to judge everything by eye. Near the end of the job the foreman asked me to make my last visit on a Friday and make it my last visit of the day. When I arrived, the foreman said he wanted to take me to the pub as a thank you for always arriving promptly and helping to make the job finish early.

He told me he had phoned my boss and agreed everything, and he asked me if I would like to move my bike inside the site. Here it would be kept undercover and would be locked in. I wasn't using my bike that weekend, so I agreed. I phoned my office to make sure that all was well, and my boss told me to enjoy myself. The foreman, a few labourers and I, went to the pub and the foreman produced from his back pocket, a roll of banknotes bigger than anything I had ever seen before. I had a pub meal and the foreman bought drinks for the whole evening. I was glad that I had decided to go home by train because, when I left, I couldn't even walk in a straight line, let alone ride my motorbike.

The previous year I had got my HNC. This year I was doing my HNC endorsements which were meant to make it equivalent to a university degree. Unbeknownst to me, that year the Institute of Civil Engineers had changed their membership policy. I applied for membership and they said they were only accepting applications from degree candidates. After studying for five years for ONC, HNC and HNC endorsements, I felt annoyed and betrayed, so I changed my employers and my career. I joined the civil service as a trainee computer programmer.

A few years after I left the GLC, it was dissolved. Many years later, it was resurrected as the GLA, led by Ken Livingstone and latterly by Boris Johnson. After nine arduous months of interviews and exams, I joined the Metropolitan Police Service (MPS). When I joined the MPS they were a combined computing department with the home office and were called 'Joint automatic data processing unit' (JADPU). When the home office relocated to Merseyside, we changed our name to 'Department of Computing Services' (DCS).

Many years later we changed our name again, for reasons best known to the senior management. We became DOT 'Department of Technology', although I failed to see what technology we offered, besides computing. You might say that to change our name, just to put a feather in the cap of our director, was just being cynical... or was it?

Initially, I was trained as both a basic and a Cobol programmer and soon I was programming for real. I stayed at MPS for twenty-one years. Some may call this excessive, but I performed a multitude of roles. I programmed for two years and then I was foolish enough to listen to a senior member of staff. She suggested that I would make a good operator.

I only worked for two weeks at New Scotland Yard, but I heard two amusing stories. Firstly, a group of Japanese tourists, all equipped with cameras, wandered past the security guard unnoticed. They then entered one of the lifts, went to a floor that they had no right to be on and took copious photos. They were finally discovered and returned to the reception, where a very embarrassed security guard took the films from their cameras and sent them on their way.

On another occasion, a diminutive female operator saw a commander trying to gain access to the computer room without using the code. He was trying to sneak in behind someone else. Seeing the possible breach of security, she rugby tackled him to the ground. He was so annoyed that he tried to have her sacked. Fortunately, the computer manager gave her his full backing and caused such a fuss that the commander had to apologise to the commissioner.

Two weeks later, I was asked to set up a new computer room at Jubilee House, Putney. I was confronted by an empty room and my brief was, to take delivery of the computer equipment and oversee its installation. I also took delivery of the office furniture and I engaged two shifts of three operators each. Soon we were operational.

I came in, just before 11.00am, on the late shift and found a message to phone Miss Spencer on an internal home office number, as a matter of urgency. A very posh voice answered, and when I asked if Miss Spencer worked there, there was a slight delay and he said, 'we don't have a Miss Spencer working here, but there is a Miss Spencer living here; most people call her Lady Diana.'

I apologised for interrupting him and said I had just realised it was April the first. His last words were, 'very droll Sir'.

When I replaced the receiver, my colleagues were all laughing, and I realised, that somehow they had found the internal number for Clarence House. It was the best April fool I had ever been the victim of.

Nearby, was another computer room which housed the most sensitive computer, serving some, very, high- ranking detectives, and holding information on some very high-profile criminals. One day, one of the operators was getting bored, so he decided to swing on the door of the main processor. The hinges were not designed for his weight, so they gave way and he fell to the floor with the door on top of him. As he fell, he reached out his hand and switched off the processor.

The shift leader came to investigate. When he saw the operator lying on the floor, he said, 'silly boy', or words to that effect. Just at that moment all the phones started ringing. The shift leader picked up the nearest phone and found he was talking to the Detective Superintendent. Unable to tell him the truth, he told him that a component in the processor had suddenly and most unexpectedly failed. He promised that the component would be replaced, and the system made available within a few minutes. After he replaced the receiver, he said something to the operator which is unrepeatable, but sounded most painful.

I enjoyed the setting up of the computer room, but I found the day to day running tedious. Desperate to escape, I was willing to accept the first vacancy offered. It was a big mistake, because the work in the new position was extremely boring. I decided to make the job more interesting by volunteering to investigate ways of reducing the department's computer maintenance bill. I decided to target our main supplier and I nominated myself on the first large scale, third party maintenance conference. It was soon discovered who I represented, which made an eventful lunch.

On my left was a representative from one of the largest third-party maintainers. On my right was a representative from our main suppliers. Each was trying to extol their own virtues. I had every intention of leaving the maintenance with our supplier, but I wanted to use the threat of the third- party maintenance, as a weapon against them. Having obtained a substantial discount from them, I moved on.

Finally, I escaped my period of purgatory and joined the

Installation Planning Team. It was a new branch and, for some reason was given the number of dcs16(0), so we were nicknamed the zero boys. I hope this didn't reflect the amount of work we did. Our main responsibility was the planning of major installations and the purchase of medium sized pieces of equipment or systems. I took a course in Systems Analysis which helped me to write operational requirements. These were very detailed documents which reflected the exact needs of the customer. The biggest system I implemented was a statistical system for G10 branch. The company who won the contract was Microdata, based in Dunstable. I spent a week with their chief designer helping with the system.

We were lucky enough to have a trolley service twice a day. The trolley held sandwiches, snacks and two urns. One of the urns contained boiling water for tea the other contained coffee. One of our tea ladies was very absentminded and would often pour coffee on top of a teabag. If you were lucky, you could pour it away and ask for another. If you were unlucky, you didn't notice until you tasted it. It was disgusting!

One character in our department was an operator named Everton. He would come out with statements which were funny but not thought through. Once, in a pub, he was asked what he would like to drink. He said, 'I'll have a scotch on the rocks with ice.'

Another time, he was asked if he wanted to go to lunch. He said, 'I'm much too hungry to think about eating.'

In the mid 1980's Roger Gregory joined DCS as director. In my opinion he was the best thing that ever happened to the department. He was a breath of fresh air, with his apparent interest in the work of all branches, and his phenomenal memory for names. Several years later, he was promoted to the rank of Deputy Receiver for the M.P.S. This rank was subsequently abolished, and he was made redundant. Some would say that his premature demise was orchestrated; all I can say is that the M.P.S. lost a good – perhaps great, man.

I joined the CRIS, Crime Report Information Service team, but worked on the ILMCS,Inner London Magistrate Court Service project. The project involved the installation of a computer at each court, running EQUIS, which was designed by Sound Techniques of Mildenhall. EQUIS allowed each court to communicate with the associated police stations. Each police station could input charges and summons directly to the court using an X25 network and dumb terminals. For those of you unfamiliar with the term 'X25' think of it as like the M25 but replacing cars with packets of data but moving much faster. This replaced typewriters and pony express. I had been promoted by then, so I became the police Project Manager.

While I was working on the project, I became friends with a superintendent called Dave. One day, Dave told me the story of his first arrest. He was fresh out of training college and was being driven by his Sergeant in a Panda car. Although they were on a night shift, and it was dark, Dave was sure that he spotted a personal attack going on at the end of a cul-de-sac.

The Sergeant drove them along the cul-de-sac and the headlights revealed that the perpetrator was one of the Kray gang. The man's weapon of choice was a meat cleaver and he was using it to cut the buttons off his victims' shirt and no doubt intended to cause further harm to him. The sergeant looked at Dave and said, 'Arrest that man.'

Dave got out of the car and approached the scene with much trepidation. Then, like a scene from Dixon of Dock Green, he tapped the aggressor on the shoulder and said, 'I arrest you in the name of the law.'

To Dave's surprise, the felon, turned around, dropped the cleaver, held out his wrists and said, 'It's a fair cop Guv.'

In those days a villain would never dream of harming a Policeman.

The project ran for three and a- half years and finished on time, on budget and fulfilled a hundred percent of the used requirements. EQUIS was a good system but had many deficiencies. I devised a system which I called PORTEUS (provision of replacement terminals for EQUIS users). It allowed a whole charge or summons to be input on a PC. This gave the user on-screen validation and edit facilities.

During the first few weeks, I worked closely with Paul Hopfensberger to help him design PORTEUS. Jane Sawtel came to work for me, training the users on EQUIS with aplomb, and stayed with me to retrain the customers in the use of PORTEUS. The new system was easier to use but was more complex. The PORTEUS project ran until 1996 and finished on time and on budget. I deliberately left the contract loose so we could take advantage of emerging technology. It was more than the user expectations.

Geoff Frost, the managing Director of Sound Techniques, and Bob Steel, the Director of Finance, invited Jeff Lock, who was my boss, and I, for a celebratory lunch. I ordered the wild boar and, as I had never tried it, I waited in eager anticipation. On the way to our table the waiter tripped and threw my dinner all over my new jacket. The boar may have been wild, but I was furious! Fortunately, my dry cleaner was able to remove the stain.

After the PORTEUS project had ended, I joined the rest of the CRIS team as the new software test manager. I was responsible for the testing of all fixes and changes prior to release. Jane helped me with the testing and Dave Gibb joined me to do the same. I believe there are only two types of testing for changes, whatever the size of the change. They are, what I call, positive and negative testing. With positive testing, you ensure that the new software does what you expect. With the negative testing, you ensure that it has no ill effects on the other software.

Before I continue, I should explain that both James and Mike worked for the CRIS suppliers, Electronic Data Systems (EDS) and although James worked for Mike, they had also been good friends for many years and would often ridicule each other. One extremely large change was proposed, so we called a meeting with the supplier. James, who was responsible for the change, came along to the meeting to explain it. James suffered from an acute stammer, made worse by nerves. That day it was particularly bad, and he stumbled through the explanation. When he had, at last, finished, Mike looked at him and said, 'well that's easy for you to say.'

While I was test manager, I responded to a job advertisement for a position at Sainsburys head office. It was doing the same job for twice the salary. Having passed the paper sift, I was called for an interview. I was not very experienced with job interviews, so I was thoroughly nervous. However, on the morning, I woke up to a blue sky and I felt supremely confident. The interview was easy, and although long, I had them eating out of the palm of my hand. I was shortlisted and called for a second interview.

Sadly, the day before the interview my girlfriend, Kim, left me, with no explanation, and after what had been, a long-term relationship. I was shocked and the next day I did an appalling interview so, not surprisingly, I did not get the job.

At the de-briefing, I was told that they shortlisted only two people and I was the favoured candidate. However, my interview was so bad that they had given the job to the other person. I was asked what had happened because they noticed that all my confidence and assertiveness had abandoned me. I explained what had happened and the interviewer said, I should have said something before, and they would have re-scheduled the interview. As the French say, 'c'est la vie'!

Bob, one of my colleagues, had never been noted for his diplomacy but one day he was tactless, even by his own stand-ards. Through the open office doorway, he saw Mark, a senior manager walking along the corridor with the director. Mark was nearly seven feet tall and the director was just over five feet. Bob poked his head out of the door and shouted, 'Hey Mark, who's your dwarf friend?'

To my knowledge, he wasn't even disciplined. Bob seemed to be able to say what he liked with complete impunity. Of course, he may have been reprimanded in private, but to Bob it would have been like water off a ducks' back. On another occasion, a friend of Bob's, named Tony, had resigned, and his leaving card was being circulated. Most people had written pleasantries such as 'good luck in your new job' or, 'we will miss you'. Bob wrote, 'good riddance and don't come back.'

Very few people understood Bob's sense of humour but fortunately for him, Tony was one who did.

During an extended slack period, Tony Sully started Superstars.

It was a contest which involved several 'sporty' events and about twenty people. Some of the events were fairly serious, like table tennis, or running. Others were more light- hearted, like welly throwing, or speed drinking through a straw. To demonstrate my level of fitness and sporting prowess, the only event I won, was speed drinking beer through a straw.

The Police staff of the CRIS team were gradually taking over all software testing, so I joined the Implementation team, with Ian Holden at the helm. Their responsibility was to survey all Police premises assessing the CRIS equipment and cabling requirements. They would then install and test all the equipment. Most of the premises were police stations, but some were offices. The team had completed most of the surveys, but no one had been to Windsor Castle, which was due to have one CRIS terminal.

Dave and I decided to go there suitably attired. Because it was Windsor Castle, we decided to leave our cars behind and instead to ask Alan to chauffer us there in his black limo. He wore his chauffers' uniform, complete with cap. When we arrived, we were allowed into the inner carpark because we were on official business. As we left, the Changing of the Guards was about to start, a crowd of tourist, mainly Japanese, had gathered to watch. They saw us in our chauffer driven limo and must have thought we were royalty for they started taking photos. We gave a royal wave and I'm sure they went home wondering who we were.

Dave and I joined a local gym,, which we frequented for a year. It was managed by a very nice chap called Richard, and because the gym was very small, he sometimes doubled as a personal trainer. One day Richard announced that he was leaving the gym to spend more time with his little band who were doing quite well. As it transpired the term 'doing quite well' was a huge understatement. To my surprise, a short while later, I saw Richard on Top of the Pops and his band was number one in the pop charts. His little band was called 'Right said Fred.'

On one summer's day, several of us were installing equipment at Catford Police station. It was tea break time and it was Karl's turn to fetch the drinks. As it was a hot day, we all asked for cold drinks. When Karl asked what I wanted, I asked for a normal Coke. Karl looked at my stomach and asked, 'have you considered a diet Coke?'

In the year 2000, six of us were outsourced to a big American company. For the first two years we continued working on the CRIS contract, installing equipment. This contract was very important to them and we had local knowledge, skills and security clearance which none of their other staff had, so they treated us like VIPs'. We received bonus', gifts, Champagne and an extravagant meal every two months. I once, jokingly, said to my boss, 'oh no boss not another meal.'

After two years were up, three things had happened:

1, The terrorist attack on the Twin Towers which affected all American companies.

2, Our CEO was rash enough to say to the press that the company was not doing at all well and had decided not to take on any new business. Overnight the share price plummeted to a tenth of its' original price.

3, The CRIS rollout had ended.

The company had a completely different attitude towards us and told us to find our own contracts to work on. This came as quite a shock to us ex-civil servants, but Dave and I applied to work on the Royal Courts of Justice (RCJ) account. When I went for my interview, I was very hirsute as I had grown my hair and a full beard for the part of Tevye, the Topol part, in Fiddler on the roof. The show ended on a Saturday and on the Sunday, I did a sponsored head shave. When I started work at the RCJ, I was completely bald and clean shaven. No one knew who I was, and who could blame them? I had transformed from Dave Lee Travis to Kojak.

It was a lovely building to work in, but all Dave and I did was man the phones. Sometimes, if the job was fairly straightforward, whoever took the call would leave the office and attend the Judge or Clerk. One day, I was fixing a Clerks' PC and he said that his Judge had just heard the case of Michael Douglas and Catherine Zeta Jones. They had brought their case to the RCJ because a magazine had published their wedding photographs without their knowledge or consent. The Judge didn't know who either of them was. Michael Douglas just laughed it off, but Catherine Zeta Jones was less amused.

Another time, I was upgrading the PC for a Judge. He said that he had to hear a case in half an hour so he would be leaving the office. We were on the fourth floor and. ten minutes later, a commotion broke out below. The Judge beckoned me to join him at the window, so I asked what was going on. He replied, 'I don't know I'll have a better look.'

With that, he reached into a drawer and produced a large pair of binoculars. When he had taken a look, I asked again what was going on. He replied, 'I don't know, but I hope it's not the case I am trying in twenty minutes.'

While I was at the RCJ I photographed the official opening of the Gym. The Gym company asked Lord Wolfe, The Lord Chief Justice, and Lord Phillips, The Master of the Rolls, to officiate and, they asked me to take photographs. Several of the Judiciary also came to watch. Lord Wolfe was very reserved, so after I had photographed him cutting the ribbon, I could only persuade him to put one hand on one of the bikes. Some of the more extravert Judges posed for me on the rowing machines, or the bikes.

When it came to the speech Lord Wolfe, deferred to Lord Phillips, who was an experienced speaker. His speech was excellent and started with this, 'There are many advantages in being asked to open a Gym. Harry and I have been given free membership for a year' He then clutched his stomach and added, 'so I truly can be the Master of the Rolls.'

When Dave and I first joined the RCJ, we were offered training to learn more about computers and then be able to offer a second line support. A year later we had received no training. So, Dave asked for early retirement and I asked for a transfer to an account that needed a Project Manager. It took a long time, but I got my transfer and became a Regional Delivery Manager (RDM). My head office was in Telford and my boss was Caroline Scholey, who was one of the best bosses I had had in 30 years. I only had to go to Telford once a month for a meeting. I would leave home at 6 a.m. to beat the traffic, and the congestion charge. I would then drive through the middle of London, stopping on the M6 for breakfast.

The position of RDM attracted a company car, which presented them with a problem. I was still on a civil service contract, which didn't allow for a company car. In the short term I used my car and claimed the mileage, but finally they came up with a solution. I was told to hire a car from Avis and claim it as an expense.

I was first allocated as an RDM to the prison service account. My responsibility was to replace all the equipment in the prisons in the South of England. It was a 'baptism of fire', when I attended Wandsworth prison. I was standing next to the guard's office which overlooked each wing. Suddenly, a riot started which was serious enough to put six guards in hospital. Several officers came from nowhere and ran into a wing without closing the gate. I was acutely aware that if some of the prisoners made a dash for the gate, I would be the only person standing between them and freedom!

I was told, later, that the gate was left open intentionally to allow additional officers to enter a wing without delay. Furthermore, I was assured that if any prisoners had made a bid to escape the guard would have reached the gate first and shut it.

The words were not very comforting. I arranged the replacement of equipment in a few more prisons and then I was transferred to the Department of Works and Pensions (DWP). They needed an RDM to manage the relocation of John Hutton, The Secretary of State, and his entire office from one London building to another. This was a hundred and twenty members of staff, in all. The move was to be arranged over Christmas, with zero tolerance and zero downtime. This was a tall order for my team, especially as we were working around building contractors, furnishing people, and BT.

The only way to achieve our aim was to supply additional equipment and make the new offices operational prior to the move. Computer bases were easy to find, but not so the screens. A girl from head office said she could source a hundred and twenty flat screens, which she promised me. The next time I went to head office, the girl admitted that she had given the screens to someone else. I was furious and told her so in no uncertain terms. I apologise for always calling her 'the girl' but I must have erased her name from my memory!

She went running to Caroline's boss, who happened to be her sister. I was called into the big boss's office, torn off a strip for my language and told to apologise. When I emerged from her office Caroline told me not to worry. She then marched into her boss's office and shut the door. I don't know what was said, I only know that I got my screens and nothing more was said about it.

The new accommodation was ready on time and fully operational. John Hutton was delighted and laid on a champagne reception for all of us. He didn't come himself, but he sent a senior civil servant to look after us.

The last account I worked on was British Petroleum. It was a strange situation for me. Caroline was still my boss, but all my work came from Carl. My first job, at very short notice, was an international conference for Tony Hayward,CEO of BP. BT arranged the audio-visual, and it was my job to have my team take international emails and convey them to the floor.

The head of BP's IT section insisted that we use the wireless network. My engineer wasn't at all confident that it would be robust enough to withstand the demands of everyone wanting to watch the conference.

Sure enough, when people started to come into work and login the network became slower. Fortunately, I had hidden a wired network under the desk. Five minutes before the conference was due to start the wireless network failed completely. We connected to the wired network and were operational twenty seconds before the conference started. The next day we received an email from the head of IT saying that Tony Hayward was extremely pleased with the way the conference had gone and wished to convey his thanks to all concerned. The head of IT added that the whole event had gone so smoothly, he wondered why we were needed!

As I was a longstanding customer of Avis, I was offered a free upgrade to a Saab 93 twin turbo Sport. It was a lovely car and wonderful to drive but it made me realise the disadvantage of hiring a car. Whenever I went on holiday, I would have to give it back. Avis told me that if I returned the Saab, I may not get it back because they only had one and it was very sought after. My wife, Liz and I were due to go to France for two weeks, so I put it on private hire and drove it to France. When we returned, I put it back on company hire.

By the recession of 2008, the company's share price hadn't rallied by much. The company's senior management reacted by taking away our cars, stopping the payment of all future expenses and telling us to attend all remote meetings, both internal and with the customer, by phone. This made it very difficult to do my job.

Inevitably, in its weakened state, the company was taken over by a larger company. The new company was keen to get rid of 'dinosaurs' like me, so they offered several of us, voluntary redundancy. I was hanging on to my civil service contract and I was just over 50, so they had to offer me an early retirement package. The offer was quite reasonable, and I was becoming disenchanted with my employment, so, in January 2009 I accepted. Besides, I was sure I could build my wedding photography business. The effects of the recession, and the introduction of the digital camera, were things I hadn't bargained for.

I realise that you should never end a sentence with a preposition, such as 'for', but it reminds me of a sentence that Sir Winston Churchill supposedly used to demonstrate just how inflexible are the rules of the English language. The sentence is perfectly constructed, grammatically correct and obeys all the rules, but it sounds ridiculous. He said, 'this is a situation up with which I will not put'.

The recession caused most couples to cut back on the cost of their weddings. The advent of the digital camera meant most couples had a friend or relative who had a nice camera and who was a self-appointed professional photographer. Of course, some couples will end up with a good set of photographs – it was, after all, how I started. However, most couples will be very disappointed. In due course, couples will realise the error of their friends' ways and return to the professional photographer. In the meantime, instead of building my business, my numbers were reduced considerably. The only saving grace was that, when I had the stroke, there were very few bookings to cancel. I now regard myself as fully retired.

'I love work – I could watch it all day'.

Chapter 16

Let them eat cake

One day my boss brought in her copy of Jane Asher's book of cake creations. I looked at her book and flippantly said, 'I wouldn't mind making one of those one day.'

Her reaction couldn't have been more dismissive, and she said I couldn't possibly make any of those designs. It was like a red rag to a bull. I bought my own copy of her book and attempted two of her more difficult designs.

No one told me you could buy fondant icing from a supermarket, so I tried to make my own. I used white fat and icing sugar. I hadn't heard of indirect heating whereby ingredients were placed in a bowl which is suspended over a saucepan of boiling water. Instead I tried heating the fat in a saucepan. I threw away the lot before I finally made a batch that you could roll and manipulate without it cracking. I found a recipe for a rich fruit cake and I injected it with brandy. It took three months, but I finished the two designs.

I then, photographed them, and took the photos in to show my boss. She wouldn't accept that I had made them and called me a liar, saying that either my mum, or sister must have made them. It started as an exercise just to prove to myself that I could do it, but I thoroughly enjoyed it, so I started making my own designs. I went to two classes to learn some of the more difficult techniques, such as making edible flowers and weaving with flowers. I was quite a novelty, being the only man in the class.

Every Christmas my nephews would eagerly wait to see 'Uncle Paul's' latest design. I made a lot of Christmas cakes, but my favourite was probably Santa Claus climbing onto the cake and spilling his sack of toys.

Each present was a small piece of cake wrapped in marzipan and icing. This was then piped with icing string which was then painted gold. There was also a teddy bear, which was not wrapped and was made of marzipan.

I assembled a selection of tools and accessories. They included a thick plastic cake maker's sheet, a small rolling pin, a set of small plastic tools for kneading and cutting, a syringe for injecting brandy, various food colours, icing bags, scalpels, and a set of piping nozzles. I also put myself on a couple of courses to learn the techniques that I hadn't yet mastered. These included making and working with royal icing. Making flowers with icing and piping including lattice work. I started making cakes for other occasions such as christenings, weddings and birthdays.

I once made a cake for Sue's son Ed's birthday. He was a firefighter, so I made a yellow firefighter's helmet, with eyes, nose and feet.

Another occasion for which I made a cake was the 40th wedding anniversary of Iona and John. It depicted a cricket pitch as John's major passion was cricket, and butterflies, these being a favourite of Iona. The cake was square with a red rose at each corner.

Chapter 17

1996 – a momentous year

1996 turned out to be a momentous year for me. Kim and I were invited to the wedding of Megan, her best friend who was marrying Mark in the village of Echtingham, West Sussex. It was a long way from where the couple lived, but it was where Megan grew up. They had a professional photographer, but he didn't have a backup photographer, so Megan asked me to take a few photos over his shoulder. This placed me in an awkward position, because I felt I was very much an amateur, but I agreed to do it.

A week before the wedding, the photographer broke his hand playing football, so I received a frantic phone call from Megan asking if I would take over. My camera was fairly good, but I didn't think it was good enough, so I borrowed a Canon Eos10. I spent a few days familiarising with the controls and by the day of the wedding I felt fairly confident. I took nine films and I was pleased with the results. Several of the couple's friends saw the photos and I began receiving phone calls asking if I would photograph their weddings. On each occasion, I explained that it was a favour to Megan, and I didn't have a business. One bride to be said, 'perhaps you should consider it.'

This is how Paul Allen Wedding Photography was born. I traded until I had my stroke in 2012. In those sixteen years, I must have photographed nearly 200 weddings. Most of my clients have been delighted with the services I offered and the final results. However, I received three complaints. One groom said I took too many photos and made it difficult to choose. I have always preferred to spoil my clients for choice rather than offer no choice. I offered him a good price for all the photos and eventually he accepted.

One bride, said I was charging the balance too late. This was after they had returned from their honeymoon having overspent. I used to charge the balance on delivery of the photos, but that was soon rectified. In accordance with all other photographers, I started charging the balance two weeks before the wedding. It seemed immoral but it followed industry standard.

The last complaint didn't come from the couple, who seemed delighted with the results. It came from the bride's mother, who sent me a letter a month after the wedding accusing me of missing a vital photo. This was despite the fact that it was not included in the 90 photos which the couple had asked for. It wasn't asked for on the day of the wedding and wasn't even thought of until a month later. I have always tried very hard to give the couples exactly what they want. but one thing I have never been very good at is mind reading.

Over the years I have photographed weddings at prestigious venues including the Alexandra Palace, Buxton Palace, Eltham Palace and the Ritz Hotel.

When I surveyed the Ritz with the couple, the bride's parents came too. We tried to cross the restaurant to look at the patio, but the bride's father was told he had to wear a tie. He was then lent a tie, which made him look ridiculous because he was wearing a donkey jacket.

I have also photographed some military weddings including a member of the Scots guards. The couple were married at the Wellington Barracks, which is opposite Buckingham Palace. I like to joke that I photographed Kate Middleton's first wedding. Of course, it was not THAT Kate Middleton, but she was marrying a captain in the RAF. I met the groom in the George pub opposite the Royal Courts of Justice. He was with his best man and ushers, all of whom were also captains in the RAF, and in uniform. One of the ushers was a bit late and one of his friends said, the country gives you one of the fastest planes on earth and you are still late. He protested, saying that he didn't come by plane.

I did a remake of the photo of the Beatles on the cover of their Abbey Road album. Instead of the four Beatles crossing Abbey Road, I had several officers crossing the Strand. I had to the stop the traffic and when I turned around to apologise the driver at the front of the queue said that it was fine because he was taking his own photo with his phone.

The couple were married at St. Clement Danes, which is the RAF headquarters church and looks like a small cathedral inside. When the bride arrived with her father the officers did something I have never seen before. They formed two lines and gave a guard of honour salute, which is standing to attention with their swords vertically in the air.

When the couple emerged from the Church, they gave a more traditional guard of honour with their swords forming an arch for the couple to walk under. The last two officers lowered their swords to stop the couple from leaving the arch, until they had kissed. It made a lovely photograph. Next, I asked Kate to lie across the hands of all the officers. Kate was very petite so the officer on the end had nothing to support. He shouted to the groom, 'here Al, you need a longer bride.'

They held their reception at the RAF officers club, at Piccadilly, so we stopped, 'en route', to take some photos at St James Park.

I have been the photographer at many cosmopolitan weddings. Such as a Jamaican woman, marrying a Japanese man, and a Jamaican bride, and a Russian groom. At the reception of the latter wedding there was no wine just several bottles of rum and vodka. I have also photographed a diminutive Indian bride, and an Irish rugby player.

Over the years, I have been hired by some wonderful clients, but one of my favourite weddings was that of Fabiola and Eibar.

Fabiola was half Venezuelan. Her Venezuelan mother Dalia, a Plastic and Reconstructive Surgeon, was a lovely lady and appreciated my work very much. Her English father, Michael, was a barrister and had his chambers at Lincoln's Inn where the couple held their reception. The day started at the parents' house in North London. We then went to St Clement Danes for a wonderful wedding ceremony. The buildings of Lincolns Inn made a magnificent background to my photographs. The reception was held in the small hall which was very elegant indeed. Eibar was Mexican and had asked Fabiola to find a Mariachi band for their wedding, as it was a Mexican tradition. Fabiola said that it was impossible to find one in England and then secretly booked one. I was privy to the secret, so I was able to capture Eibar's reaction as they came in singing and playing. Then I photographed the band.

Throughout the reception, individuals from the Mexican

contingent asked me if I wanted tequila. To each one I said I wouldn't have one while I was working, but I would be pleased to accept after I had finished. As I was putting my cameras away, there was a tap on my shoulder and a Mexican pointed to the six tequilas which were lined up on the bar for me. It was just as well that Liz was driving because after I had drunk six tequilas in quick succession. I couldn't even find the car let alone drive it.

At one of the weddings I photographed, there was a contingent of ten Italians, and in the evening, they all occupied a large round table. After I had photographed the top table, I went to the Italian Table. Just for fun I counted in Italian before I took the picture. On hearing this, the next table insisted I use a different language for them. Word soon spread and every table wanted a different language.

After the seventh table, I had run out of languages, but when I came to the eighth table, I remembered my Karate lessons. I counted in Japanese. When I came to leave, I said goodbye to everyone on the top table and then, as is my tradition, I said goodbye to the other tables. I decided to say goodbye in each tables' appointed language. When I came to the eighth table a 'smart uncle' asked, 'what are you going to do now?'

Without hesitation, I bowed from the waist and said 'Sayonara.'

At another wedding, the father of the bride wandered off and was nowhere to be found. When he finally returned the mother of the bride wanted me to take all the photos involving him again. As I was using film, I was not impressed. At another wedding many of the people were Actuaries, including the

Bride, Groom, the Brides' Father and the best man. During his speech the best man said, 'for those of you who don't know what an Actuary is, it is a career you should choose if you wanted to be an accountant, but found the prospect, a little too exciting.'

Apologies to all actuaries and accountants, it was a joke.

From the year 2000, Liz was my back up photographer. She would also assemble all the necessary people for each photograph. When I converted to digital cameras and could afford to take unlimited photos, I encouraged Liz to take photos freely. In many respects she worked harder than I did, but don't tell her because she'll be wanting a back dated pay rise.

I once had the privilege of photographing a centenarian on her one hundreth birthday. After she had drunk two glasses of champagne in quick succession, I said, 'Bridget, promise me you won't drive home later.'

Chapter 18

Thank you for being a friend

I am fortunate enough to have a wide circle of friends. They are from school, work, and the church, as well as from the world of music and from operatics. However, there are certain people I wished I had kept in touch with from school, work and some of my biking friends. When I was eight or nine my best friend was Ian Weight. We used to play almost every day and it was he who introduced me to the church choir.

When we were both eleven, we challenged each other to a bicycle time trial using my bike and my watch. The object was to ride as fast as possible from the closed end of a cul-de-sac to the open end. When it was my turn, I was so determined to beat Ian's time that I didn't notice the pothole at the mouth of the cul-de-sac. My front wheel went into the pothole and I flew over the handlebars, trying to stop the road with my face. When Ian saw me fly over the handlebars, he threw down the watch and rushed to my aid. When the watch hit the ground, it broke and stopped showing that I had beaten his time by two seconds. It was fortunate that the road was quiet, and nothing was coming, but I broke one front tooth in half, chipped another and made a mess of my face.

All I could think of was how I would look on the TV in a few months' time when there was a documentary being made about Archbishop Ramsey,

'Oh vanity, thy name is man', or in my case 'boy.'

By the time the TV crew descended on my church, my dentist had fitted a crown and, my face was back to normal – normal for me at least.

Ian and I, also frequented Fairfield Halls to watch the wrestling. We were always excited when we left but one particular evening, we saw our bus just arriving at its stop on the other side of the road. Ian ran across the exit from the underpass without looking. He was lucky and nothing hit him. I was less fortunate, and I slammed my hands against the side of a car. If I had been running faster, I would have been under the car. Fortunately, I had never been an athlete and I couldn't run any faster. As it was, I spun around and fell on the pavement. Ian returned to assist me, and we missed the bus. A short while later, Ian's parents moved, and I never saw him again.

During the third year of Ashburton, one of my friends emigrated with his parents to Australia. Many years later my mother's friend visited Australia for the first time to see her daughter. On the first day she went into a chemist to stock up. She was served by a young English man, so she asked where he came from. When he said Croydon, she rather optimistically said 'you must know my friends' son, Paul Allen'.

To her surprise, he said 'yes, he was one of my friends.'

It certainly is a small world.

Two of my friends were Chaz and Alan. Although they had known each other for some time they couldn't be more different. Chaz was a solicitor and Alan was mad. Likeable but mad.

Somehow, Alan got himself a job delivering new cars. He once took me for a ride in a brand new, Toyota Land Cruiser. He sped down a very narrow lane, collecting branches on his mirrors. He was finally sacked, probably for damaging a new vehicle.

Before the introduction of the Breathalyzer, Alan used to regularly drink and drive. One day coming home from the pub, he was driving far too fast on a very wet road. He tried to take a sharp right- hand bend, slid on the road, hit the kerb and turned the car upside down. He then proceeded to plough through three gardens demolishing the fences.

The owner of the last property came to ask if he was alright. Miraculously he climbed out of the car unscathed and the lady made him a cup of tea. When the police arrived, the sergeant asked who was driving and Alan said that he was. When the policeman asked him how fast he was going he said 30mph. the policeman couldn't believe that he could do so much damage at 30mph. Alan said,

'It's a heavy car officer.'

One friend I miss is Chris Rogers. He went to work for a big hi-fi manufacturer based in Birmingham, so he moved, and I haven't seen him since. He told me once that the slogan 'speed kills' isn't necessarily true. He used to race motorbikes for a local dealer. He was racing in the Isle of Man and was doing 120mph, when his front tyre burst. As he flew through the air he was heading for a stone wall and hoping he would make it through the open gate. He did, slid on the grass and only suffered minor friction burns. A few weeks later, he was riding his road bike at 30mph when, a bus pulled out in front of him. He awoke in hospital with a concussion and several broken bones. He said, 'it's not the speed you are doing, it's what you hit!'

When I used to rent a flat in Miss Andrews house, a friend of mine was Tim Marshall who occupied one of the other flats. One day he invited me to have Sunday lunch at his parents' house. They had one other guest called Peggy Sorensen. She was fascinating and, amongst other things, she spoke of the money she had wasted on three separate roofers, who tried in vain, to repair her leaking roof. I was a surveyor at the time so I said I would take a look. I went to her cottage in Hampton Hill and she showed me where it leaked inside. I went up on the roof to have a look and when I came down, I told her all the roofers had done an excellent job of repairing the wrong bit of roof. She asked if I could do the job. I said that I was a surveyor, not a roofer, but I was fairly good at DIY so I said I would try.

The following weekend I returned to Peggy's house, stopping on route at a builder's merchant to buy a length of zinc flashing and a bag of ready mixed sand and cement. I then spent the rest of the day on Peggy's roof. I worked very slowly because I had only rudimentary tools and I was struggling to put theory into practice. When I finally came down from the roof, Peggy offered to pay me but as I was not a roofer, I couldn't guarantee the job, I only charged for materials. Three days later it rained convincingly so when Peggy phoned me, I feared the worst. She said that she was extremely pleased that, at last, her roof wasn't leaking, and she said I could stay in her cottage in Ireland free of charge anytime I wanted.

A few years later, Sue and I house sat for Peggy for a week, while she went to Ireland. We were not yet married and were so grateful for the opportunity to be together that we decided to buy her a nice present. We noticed that she was collecting Port Meirion china, so we bought her a few items which she didn't have. We also bought her a bouquet of flowers. She never saw the china and the flowers. On the motorway on her way back from Ireland, the driver of a Range Rover coming the other way, fell asleep at the wheel, crossed the central reservation and hit Peggy head on. She must have died instantly. She was a lovely lady and it was a tragic accident.

On a happier note, four of us decided to do the 'Young's round'. It entailed visiting all 135 Young's Pubs and obtaining signatures from all the landlords. Stuart was happy to drive to most of the pubs as it was a chance to drive his father's Austin Ambassador Van den Plas. On the way to one of the pubs, Colin and I were sitting on the back seat, when some piano music came over the airwaves. Colin started to pretend to play piano on one of the front seats. Suddenly, he stopped and quite profoundly said, 'I wish I had learnt to play piano – it would all mean more then'.

Most of the pubs were in Greater London, but one was at Plumpton Green, which is halfway to Brighton. The landlord of the pub explained why. John Young, the chairman of the brewery, moved to Plumpton Green to get away from London, and because it was an idyllic village. He was appalled to find that, of the two pubs in the village, one was closed and the other one, at the time, served dreadful beer. He bought the closed pub and installed a landlord. It was the landlord's job to renovate the pub and then run it. The landlord told us that on the opening day he made the mistake of opening at lunchtime. He stood at the bar for 2 hours without a soul coming through the door.

Finally, a man came in and before he could say a word the landlord said that the first pint was free. The man protested saying that he had left the main road to Brighton and was now lost. He just wanted directions to get back on the main road. The landlord gave him directions but insisted he tried the beer before he left. When the man left the pub, he bumped into a local who said that he thought the pub was closed. The man replied that not only was it open, but it served excellent beer. The local decided to look for himself and agreed that the beer was superb. He spread the word and the pub had been busy ever since.

Two of us finished the round. The reward was a Young's 135 club tie, a thirty-six- pint barrel of beer and a private guided tour around the brewery. The original four of us presented ourselves at the brewery in Wandsworth. It was the first such tour that I had ever been on, so I found it fascinating. It culminated in a trip to the sampling room. We were locked in and not allowed out until we had drunk their copious amount of beer. It was terrible!

We emerged from the brewery in high spirits, so we decided to have a trolley race, through Wandsworth. We acquired two shopping trolleys, two people sat in them and two of us pushed them. When we found a telephone box, we stopped to phone for 2 cabs. While we were waiting for the taxis, I chased Trevor around the phone box. After a while, I peeled off and left Trevor chasing himself. I'm not sure if he ever caught himself, but it looked very funny.

Colin Hoare was one of my best friends. We went for beers and curries and we once went on holiday to Cornwall. I also visited him at Southampton University, and he was one of the original four who started the Young's round. He was an agnostic, rather than an atheist, as he desperately wanted to believe in something – he just didn't know what. I invited him to my church for an evening service. I was in the choir at the time and we sang a fairly elaborate mass which he seemed to enjoy. After the service he went to shake hands with the vicar, who completely ignored him and walked straight past him. It only served to confirm his belief that he wasn't wanted in church. I tried to persuade him the church wasn't like that, we just had a weird vicar, but Colin was only interested in going for a pint.

A mutual friend called Stuart Woodrow, invited Colin and I to stay with him at Bath University in the halls of residence. On the first night we decided to go to the town and sample the local beer. We returned to the halls of residence completely inebriated. I have rarely had a fight in my entire life, but that night, in our drunken state Colin and I had one in Stuart's room.

I thought I was defending a lady's honour, but I was just being stupid. I was sure that Colin would win because he was much more advanced than me in Karate, so I hung on to his neck. We both tripped over Stuart's bed, and Colin went, head first, into the wall. He was bleeding profusely, and I should have helped him, but I turned my back and walked away. It is something I regret very much, and it has haunted me all my life. That night I lost a good friend over a pointless fight. I would very much like to see him again, but I realise that, at my time of life, it is unlikely. Particularly, because I don't even know his address now.

I have known the Websters since 1980. I first met Hazel and her daughter Diane when I joined the Hillcrest Players, but I soon became a friend of the family. Hazel's husband, Graham, helped me to spray my car and change the engine and I helped them to clear the back garden.

One day Sue and I invited them to dinner with two mutual friends, Steve Angel, and his girlfriend Anna. I knew that Steve and Anna were vegetarians, but they ate fish, so the main course was pretty much decided. I was very proud of the first course because it was vegetarian but very tasty. Hazel and Graham had declared no likes, dislikes or allergies so I thought I would be safe. The dish was similar to fisherman's pie but replacing the fish with asparagus and mushrooms. This was then covered in mushroom and cheese sauce before covering the whole dish with mashed potato. When Hazel had taken one mouthful she asked if there were any mushrooms in it. When I said, yes there were, she shouted, 'Stop Graham, don't eat that.'

She then explained that Graham was allergic to mushrooms after seven in the evening. Steve then started to ridicule Graham, asking if it was GMT or BST, and asked him what would happen if he travelled to a different time zone. Without more ado, I changed Graham's starter for something else. The main course was simple. It was a rainbow trout on a bed of wild rice, accompanied by a side salad. Having checked that no one was allergic to rainbow trout. I thought that the main course was innocuous enough to attract no further complaints.

I couldn't have been more wrong. All four plates were returned to have the fish heads removed. Sue made the desert which included a set mousse. I was just thinking that the evening couldn't get any worse, when Hazel asked Sue how she got the mousse to set so well, 'Did you use gelatine?' she asked.

Sue innocently replied that she had. Immediately the vegetarians downed tools and said that they couldn't possibly eat anything with gelatine in it. By that point, I just wanted the evening to end. It had been the most disastrous dinner party we had ever hosted. When Sue and I got divorced, Hazel stopped talking to me. I can't fathom why, since Sue and I had always been on speaking terms.

I first met Robert Hedden in about 1985, when I did Finnian's Rainbow with the South London Theatre Centre (SLTC) and Robert was the director's assistant. I met his wife, Jean, the next year when she was choreographing Godspell, also at the SLTC. A few years later they bought a villa in Ibiza and they invited Sue and me to stay for free.

One of my character defects is that if I see something broken, I have to fix it. Robert was delighted when I returned to England with a long list of things I had done and another list of things that needed to be done. He decided to formalise the arrangement and said I could go to the villa at any time in return for doing some jobs.

One year he told me that it was Jean's fiftieth birthday the next year. He had seen some of my cakes and he wanted to commission me to make her a birthday cake. I knew it was going to be a big affair because he had hired a nightclub and invited two- hundred guests.

I was at a loss how to design the cake but when I next went to the villa, I had a moment of inspiration. I would make a scale replica of the villa in cake. I took copious measurements and the design started as a two-dimensional drawing. I bought a model Suzuki Jeep by, like Robert's jeep at the Villa. It was 1-43 scale, so this determined the size of the cake. The Jeep was the wrong colour, so I took it apart and sprayed it. The cake included a pool table, swimming pool, outside bar, the garden, a flight of steps, the garage and the retaining wall. The villa had its own thin cake board so it could be removed from the cake. The villa was hollow and made from pastillage icing. This is a very hard brittle icing which is easy to model with. Having made the walls, I glued them together with royal icing. The cake was made in six parts which were joined together with jam. The whole cake was three feet long by one foot six inches wide and weighed sixty pounds, so I made a stretcher to carry it on.

Although the cake was technically, a commission, it had taken 270 hours to make. I couldn't, charge Robert, so, I decided to give it to Jean, as a birthday present. At the venue several people said it looked exactly like the villa. It should have because it was a scaled model.

I met the Payne's in 1985. Barbara directed several shows that I was in, and Keith was the stage manager. I did offer to fit a loft ladder for them but somehow, I never did. As I said to Keith, 'I didn't say I would do it one day in May, I said I may do it one day.'

I met Mark Newman in 1987, and he became my best

friend. We would meet for a few beers and a curry. Also, we went on four holidays together, two in France and two in Ibiza. In Ibiza he was the only one I know who enjoyed the inside of a hardware shop more than me.

We went to a beer festival in Dartford and he was my best man at my wedding. In 2015, sadly, he and his partner, Pat, moved to Cheshire. Mark has sold me several things including two cameras, a photo enlarger, a TV, three Swarovski pieces, his hi-fi and many other things. He always kept his belongings in immaculate condition, so I never hesitated to buy from him.

In the year 2000, I heard that Barry Ward was trying to contact me through Friends Reunited, twenty-eight years after we both left Ashburton School. I had met Ian Burgess when I was at Selhurst School and I had introduced him to Barry. They had remained friends ever since. When I contacted Barry, I arranged to meet both of them at a restaurant in South Croydon. I approached the restaurant door with much trepidation as I wondered if we would recognise each other. I decided that the best course of action was to phone Barry. When he reached for his phone, he was instantly recognisable, and when I stepped inside the restaurant so was Ian. We had a great evening and have stayed in touch, sporadically, ever since, eating in each other's homes.

In 2002, Leslie Ralph organised a class reunion to mark the thirtieth anniversary of leaving Ashburton School. It was arranged at a pub in Shirley, and was well attended. Some of my friends hadn't changed at all, but some had changed beyond all recognition. Peter Kenton used to be the shortest boy in the class, but now he towered above everyone.

In 2009, we had a Christmas dinner with Liz's work

colleagues. By sheer coincidence Liz found herself sitting next to Janet, who went to the same church at Don Mann. I had searched for many years for Don, so I resolved to see him at his church the next Sunday. On the day there was snow on the ground, but I wasn't deterred. Don knew I was coming, so when we entered the church, he gave me a warm welcome.

He looked just as I remembered. It was as if thirty-seven years had never passed. I introduced Liz, and he gave her an equally effusive welcome. He introduced his lovely wife, Heather, and we both embraced her. They were having a carol service which we both enjoyed, and we joined in with the church meal afterwards which gave Don and me plenty of time to talk. We left promising to stay in touch. When the weather was better, we invited them to our house for dinner. Shortly afterwards, they reciprocated by inviting us to theirs.

The next year, we hosted a dinner party for those who have had the greatest musical influence on me throughout my life. We invited Mike Spencer; Mike was invited because he was my church choir master from the age of ten. Jay took over from Mike as choir master when I was sixteen. I had sung with Terence in the choir for many years. I managed to contact John Vinal who I hadn't seen for thirty-nine years and his wife Angela. He was invited because he was my music master when I was eleven. He was also the musical director in the show Oliver. Don and Heather were there because Don played Fagin in Oliver and he was also the co-producer. Iona and John were invited because Iona is my singing teacher. Liz made a wonderful meal and we had a great evening. Even those who didn't know each other seemed to get on well. The evening was just too short.

Although I have mentioned my fellow artistes in Chapter seven, they also belong here, because Iona, Janet, James, Jo, Jean and Jacky are my special friends. Since my stroke they have performed a few concerts for me, including one in my Church, three at the Hospital and one at a local arts centre. It was lovely to hear them sing and I couldn't help wishing, that I could join in.

Another of my friends, Keith, the would-be recipient, of my never-quite-completed loft ladder - hired a theatre and organised several of my friends to perform a concert for me. It was like a musical, '*This is Your Life*'. It was a wonderful evening which was enjoyed by everyone.

In 2015, my friends Simon and Andrea moved to Wiltshire, Simon and Kikki moved to Norfolk, and Mark and Pat moved to Chester. Several years before, Derek and Suzette emigrated to Australia. If anymore of my friends move, or emigrate, I shall start to take it personally. Ever since my stroke, four of my friends from the metropolitan police service, Ian Holden, Eric Seers, Dave Morgan and John Chambers, have taken it in turn to visit me in hospital. Two of them, usually come every week. I was a friend of Ian long before I worked for him. I would sometimes go to his house either for social occasions, or, to borrow his power tools. My rule was that, if ever I needed the same tool twice, it was time to buy one. I have known Eric thirty-five years. He was the chairman of Ferrier Operatic Society with whom I did a number of shows starting with Fiddler on the Roof. I must have known Dave for thirty years, working with him in two branches within the Met and two contracts once we were outsourced. When we were both retired, we used to meet regularly for a drink. I used to work with John and Karl on the CRIS rollout, both within the Met and after we were outsourced.

I'm afraid this is yet another digression. It involves Brian who was a friend of my younger brother, Nigel. Brian was a chauffeur, and one day he was asked to drive an Arab Sheik. He wanted to take the job as he had heard that Arab Sheiks were very good tippers, but he had to refuse owing to previous commitments. Instead, he recommended his friend who accepted without hesitation but soon came to regret his decision.

On a rare occasion when he had an evening off, he phoned Brian to arrange to meet up for a drink. To Brian's dismay, his friend spent the whole evening saying he felt his life was no longer his own. He was on call twenty-four hours a day, seven days a week. Sometimes the Sheik would ask him to drive him to a casino late at night and expect him to wait until he was ready to come home at three or four in the morning. Other times, the Sheik would phone him to say he had a meeting, either early in the morning or late at night.

The Sheik had ordered a customized Rolls Royce to be delivered on the day of his arrival. He hadn't asked for many changes to the inside, but on the outside, he had all the chrome changed to gold! Brian's friend said the only positive side to the job was that he got to drive a Rolls Royce and on the days that he was going to the casino, he would stay at the Sheiks house. The house was more like a palace and the Sheik had bought it only for the duration of his visit.

On the last day, on the way to the airport, the Sheik thanked him for his service for the first time in three months, and when he asked what to do with the car, the Sheik said, 'keep it.'

So, after three months in purgatory, he became the proud

owner of a customized Rolls Royce Corniche. If a friend, in need, is a friend indeed I am very lucky, because a lot of good friends have visited me in my hour of need.

Chapter 19

I love my dog
(Song by Cat Stevens)

I nearly didn't write this chapter, but my story would not be complete without a mention of our pets. It is not all about dogs, as the title suggests, the name of the singer is a clue.

When I first met Liz, she had a dog, a cat, and four rabbits. Her daughter also had two chinchillas. My parents always kept a cat or a dog, but this didn't prepare me for a menagerie. Three of Liz's rabbits lived outside, but one was a house rabbit called Sidney. I called him Sid Vicious because every time I arrived wearing motorcycle gear, he would growl at me and attack my boots. I didn't know that rabbits could growl, but Sid Vicious could. He was so big he could stand on his hind legs and rest his chin on the dining room table.

The cat was called Rough and was affectionate when it suited him. Mega was a lovely Golden Retriever and she wasn't sure about me when I first arrived on the scene, but we soon became best of friends. When I was feeling low Mega would put her nose under my hand as if to say, 'stroke me and you will feel much better.'

When Liz was trying to sell the house, Sid Vicious ate a large hole in the middle of the kitchen floor. I was not impressed, so he became an outdoor rabbit living in a hutch.

When we moved to Beckenham, one of the rabbits had

died and Liz had rehomed the chinchillas. Mega, Rough and the other rabbits moved in with us. The three rabbits lived in a large hutch. I called it the rabbit town house because it consisted of three floors. I built a shed around the hutch and a picket fence around the shed, to give the rabbits somewhere safe to run around. Rabbits have very short lives so, in a few years, they were all gone.

Then came a very traumatic time. I took Mega to the vet because her left eye was troubling her. The vet wasn't sure of the diagnosis, so he referred me to a vet in Wimbledon who specialised in eyes. From the new Porsche outside her practice, the vet was doing very well. She examined Mega's eye and said that, it would trouble her no more, once it had been removed. I was so stunned that I had to ask her to repeat herself. She explained that Mega was suffering from acute glaucoma. She said that the pressure behind her eye was four times that which would make most humans scream in agony. She also said, Mega probably hadn't seen through that eye for about three months, so all she would know after the operation, was that the pain had gone.

I had a lot to think about in the tram on the way home, but because it was for Mega's good. We had the operation carried out by our vet. When Liz collected her, she looked like she belonged to Frankenstein. Her fur had been shaved around her eye, her skin was swollen and bruised, and her eyelids were stitched together. In time her fur grew back, and she was much happier. Mega used to love coming with us to Kington in Herefordshire, where Liz's mum lived, and swimming in the river. She was such a good swimmer that she could make headway against a fairly strong current. When she left the water, you had to run for cover before she shook her long fur and the water went everywhere.

As Mega grew older she slowed down a lot, so we thought that a puppy would give her a new lease of life. We bought a black Labrador. We bought her a red collar and, because she looked like the reverse of a poppy, that became her name. Unfortunately, she was a very frisky puppy and only irritated Mega.

When Poppy was young, she used to chew everything and one day I was foolish enough to leave two of my CDs on the hall stand, within easy reach. Poppy chewed both cases to the extent that the CDs were damaged. When I came home and saw what state the CDs were in, I was very angry. One CD was Nigel Kennedy playing The Four Seasons by Vivaldi and the other one was Sergeant Pepper by the Beatles. So at least it showed that Poppy had an eclectic taste in music. Although, Poppy was very irritating. Mega was very protective of her when they were outside.

One day, we took both of them to the park and removed their leads. A giant Schnauzer started to worry Poppy, so Mega positioned herself between the two dogs and warned the Snauzer away.

In due course, Mega, started to lose her sight and hearing. She also became incontinent. One day she couldn't even stand, so I carried her into the back garden. I stayed with her for a long time and I phoned Liz asking her to come home as soon as possible. When she came home, we both agreed on the 'inevitable', but we didn't want to take her to the vet. Instead, I phoned the vet and asked him to come to the house. I carried her into the lounge and waited for the vet. When he came, he said that she had only a few days to live. The veins in her legs had collapsed and she was in pain. Reluctantly, we agreed that he should end her life gracefully. We watched through the window, as the vet carried Mega to his car. It was unbearable.

Tragically, one morning, I discovered Rough's lifeless body lying in the drive. He had, presumably, been the victim of a car, or a fox. Both things would have been strange because Rough had a lot of road sense and, in a fight with a fox, you would expect him to come off best. However, we have a shortage of bears and tigers in Beckenham, so it was probably a car, or a fox. I carried him into the back garden and, when Liz came home, I broke the sad news.

A while later, we bought two kittens from Foal Farm. We were struggling over what to call them. As they were brother and sister, we decided that they should be named after a well-known duo. I suggested Purdy, from the New Avengers, because it sounded right for a girl cat. Steed didn't sound right at all, and I thought of the actor who played him, Patrick McNee. We shortened the first name to Paddy, and that became the boy cat's name. We now had a Purdy, Paddy and Poppy and they were all black!

Although the names were all similar, they all learnt their own names and they never got confused. The cats grew from cute little kittens to loveable and placid cats, or so we thought. As soon as they set foot outside, they became prolific predators, and brought back a few victims every week. Their victims ranged from mice and voles to frogs and, from birds of all sizes, including pigeons, to squirrels. Purdy usually killed her prey, but Paddy brought them back alive, as unwanted presents.

Poppy grew from a frisky little puppy, into a hyperactive big puppy. The vet diagnosed her with ADHD, which is ironic, because, Liz is a, carer, with a special needs dog! She now has a husband with special needs, as well!. The vet also recommended an additive free, low protein diet. We found the food, but it was difficult to keep Poppy on the diet because she was so greedy and often stole food. She ate sandwiches, eggs, cakes, fruit and loaves of bread to name but a few. Once she even ate a sachet of blanket weed remover. Quite why is beyond me. It said on the box that it was poisonous to children, so Liz phoned the emergency vet. The vet had a consultation with a specialist poisons unit, and they said Labradors had a cast iron constitution, so we needn't worry. They suggested that we should encourage her to drink as much water as possible and said that she might be sick.

When the pears were in season, she would wait under the tree until they dropped. Then she would catch them one by one and eat them within seconds. We thought that it would do her no harm, but sometimes she ate so many she left our lawn looking like we kept a horse. One day Poppy's special food arrived while it was pouring with rain. We normally kept it in a waterproof bin outside, but as the weather was so bad, we put it in the downstairs toilet. The food came in a fifteen kilogram sack, enough for three months. One of us must have left the door open, because that night Poppy ate half the sack. In the morning she was crying, and her belly was dragging on the ground. Liz didn't feed her for about a week, until her belly had gone down.

Another day, Poppy chewed her bed open; it was filled with polystyrene beads! I was just going to work, so I had to leave

Liz to clear up the mess! It took her two hours. One day I stepped out of the shower only to find Paddy sitting in the bath with a mouse. The little rodent was standing right up on its hind legs and jabbing with his forepaws like a boxer. Liz managed to rescue brave little mouse and released him in the garden. When Liz was preparing to move from our house, she was clearing out the cellar and found hundreds of feathers and a few birds' carcases. The cats had obviously been using the cellar as an abattoir

At the time of the actual move, Poppy was still acting like a seven- year- old puppy. She was still stealing food, but the only thing she ate which was out of the ordinary, was bird food. It made her feel chirpy, but apart from that, had no ill effects. As hunters, the cats became even more insatiable, bringing back their prey almost every day, sometimes there were two, or three, 'victims'. Liz tried telling Paddy that she didn't want any more presents, but he obviously didn't understand plain English. When Liz was talking to a friend, it transpired that he was a keen bird watcher and he said that although it was possible to see a Blackcap elsewhere, they were very rare in our area. The next time Liz saw him, she said that she had seen a Black Cap. When he asked where she had seen it, she replied, 'in the cat's mouth.'

Fortunately, it was Paddy, and when she made him release the bird it flew away, apparently unharmed. The Blackcap was nearly even rarer. Another day, Liz came home to find Purdy in the bath plucking a dead pigeon. Liz looked at her in disbelief and Purdy looked up, surrounded by feathers and, probably thinking, 'what, are you looking at? It's what cats do.' Poppy now acts like a ten-year old puppy, with no sign of slowing down. Long ago, I gave up all hope of living in a sane household.

Chapter 20

Summer Holiday

(Song by Cliff Richard)

Most of my holidays have been covered in previous chapters, but some have not been mentioned and some warrant a little more detail.

When I lived with my parents most of the family holidays were spent camping in either Cornwall, Devon or South Wales. We had a big elaborate tent with three bedrooms and a communal area. The only lighting was from a meth's burning, Tilley lamp. This was handy because, if you didn't like the light, you could always drink the meths. I'm only joking; I would never drink meths, turps is much tastier!

Our preferred destination in South Wales was the Gower Peninsular. On one family holiday, my brother Dave joined us with his friend John. One day, they buried me up to the neck in sand. If that wasn't bad enough, my younger brother, Nigel, poured a pot of cold tea over my head. It was loose- leaf tea, so it made an awful mess.

We had choir holidays in the West Country. One Sunday, some kind of insanity must have possessed me. While the others went to the pub, I volunteered to make dinner. I had never had an oven timer before, and I didn't realise it had been set. When the others returned, the chicken was not only uncooked, it was cold. Fortunately, Match of the Day was about to start, and they had brought several cans of beer, so we were all happy.

When we went to the Isle of Man, we stayed for practice and race weeks, so there was plenty of time to see the sights. We saw the Laxey Wheel, the Glens and the pubs. We were delighted to find that there was a pub just four doors away from the guest house. On the first day we parked our motorbikes and waited for them to open for lunch. We had heard that the Guinness was brewed in Dublin and that it travels well by sea, so we were keen to try it. As it took such a long time to pull, the landlord said, 'Would you like a drink while you are waiting?'

So, we all had a pint of beer.

While we were watching the races, I noticed that the man next to me had the same camera. He offered to lend me his telephoto lens, and I took some superb photos of riders coming around a distant corner.

Later that year, I spent a two- week holiday at Lands' End with Colin and two of his mates from university. We had a relaxing time, chilling on the beach, playing Frisbee and of course drinking beer.

At the end of the two weeks they decided to stay for another week because they had finished their degrees and they hadn't got jobs yet. However, I had to get back to work and, as I had not yet bought a train ticket, I decided to hitch hike. I left in the morning and by night- time I had only reached Launceston. The only drivers who had stopped were locals. It was twilight, so I jumped over a wall to get to the town. I found myself in a church graveyard, which was a bit scary, so I ran out of the grounds and headed for the nearest pub.

Once I had ordered a drink, I asked the publican if any of his customers were going to London the next day. He said they were all locals but one lady who used to work for him was now a salesperson and regularly went to London. When he phoned her, she said she was going to London the next morning and was happy to take me. The publican had an empty room, so I stayed for the night.

The next morning, I was up bright and early and, good as her word, she came to collect me. She was attractive and, although she was a lot older than me, after a few hours of talking I found her curiously interesting. At that point a small voice came from the back saying, 'Mum, are we there yet?'

All this time, her son had been asleep on the back seat and I hadn't noticed. My interest had been somewhat dampened, so I made no further advances to her. She dropped me in central London and bade me farewell. I thanked her profusely, and a tube and train ride later, I was home.

The next year Elaine and I joined Phil, Barbara and John and embarked upon our mammoth tour of Europe. We mainly, camped in the tents which we carried. If it was raining very hard, we spent the night in a hotel to allow our bike clothing to dry. The tour took four weeks, five days of which were spent in Corfu. The weather was glorious so one day Elaine and I decided to go on a ride on our own. We found a secluded restaurant where they didn't speak a word of English and they had no menu. Instead the proprietor showed us the contents of a very large fridge.

This was when I discovered we both spoke some Italian. I ordered bread and wine which were both homemade. I ordered salad which was home grown and we both had fish which was freshly caught. The food was simple but excellent. When I ordered more fish, the proprietor got very excited. She brought us two fish each, more salad, more bread and more wine. At the end of the meal we had eaten enough for six but when the bill came it was what I would expect to pay for one. After we had thanked the proprietor and left a generous tip, we went down to the beach for a rest followed by a long walk. When we returned to the bike, I still felt a bit worse for wear, but we didn't have too far to go. So, against my better judgement, I rode back to the campsite. We told our friends about the restaurant and then fell asleep. On the island we found beef tomatoes almost as big as your head, but still sweet. Beef tomatoes were unknown in the U.K, so they came as a big surprise.

In 1980, I decided to take up Peggy's kind offer to stay in her cottage in Donegal, Ireland. I had planned to go with Heather, but we had parted company just before the holiday, so I went alone. I landed in Northern Ireland, in the early hours of the morning and as soon as the Garda knew I was from England he said, 'ride and ride fast.'

I didn't know, but the previous day had been the anniversary of internment. As I rode through the streets of Derry, there were burnt out shells of what were once cars and mad dogs chasing me. I couldn't wait to leave Northern Ireland.

When I reached Peggy's cottage, it was still dark so I couldn't see the view. I awoke to a wonderful view of the sea. It was nearly lunch time, so I rode out for provisions. On the way, I asked a farmer for directions to the nearest bar. He must have thought I was going by bike because he pointed and said, 'just up that way.'

Later in the evening, I started walking towards the bar. It took hours, and I arrived at 10pm. I thought I only had an hour before I had to start walking back. Little did I know.

When I entered the bar, I was welcomed by the publican Edward Gallagher and I was befriended by a couple from Belfast who recommended black velvet. This is a mixture of Guinness and cider. The draught Guinness doesn't travel well by road, so I drank bottled. At 11pm Edward locked the door and I was amazed when at 1am the couple from Belfast said that they were just popping back for some dinner and would see me at 2am. When they returned, we were just starting a singalong. Everyone was taking it in turns to sing a song from their part of Ireland or Scotland. Suddenly, someone shouted, 'let's have a song from London.'

In my inebriated state I clapped and said, 'Yeah, a song from London.'

Edward leant over the bar and said, 'you have got to sing it, you fool.'

I sobered up quickly and thought, what do I sing from London? Then I announced that I would sing Streets of London by Ralph McTell. I didn't even know the words to that song, so three Irish girls offered to take me into the back room and teach me the lyrics. I was very embarrassed, being a Londoner and having to have three Irish girls teach me the lyrics to Streets of London. So, I wrote a verse, just for the bar. It went something like this: 'Have you seen the Londoner who walks the streets of Donegal looking for a bar that's open after one. Suddenly to his surprise he finds a bar that's just his size; its Edward Gallagher's but he's not there alone'.

The last verse went down so well, that there were cheers and I was lifted onto someone's shoulders. I didn't buy another drink for the rest of the evening. At 4am, I took my life in my hands and accepted a lift from the couple from Belfast. I'm sure he was normally a good driver but, with several drinks inside him, we spent more time off the road than on it.

Somehow, I got back to the cottage in one piece but when the daylight woke me, I was lying on a cold flagstone floor. I crawled into bed and slept for most of the day. I found that being alone in the cottage was a solitary existence, so I decided to go to Galway Bay. The cottage was in an idyllic position, but it was isolated with no immediate neighbours. I went back to Edwards bar, but this time by bike because I only intended to have one drink. I wanted to thank Edward for his hospitality the previous night and tell him I was going to Galway Bay the following day.

It was closing time when I left, so Edward locked the door. Just before I rode off, I realised that I had left my torch. I knocked on the door, not realising that it was the same as the signal used by the Garda to warn the inhabitants of a raid. Everyone clambered out of the rear windows and eventually Edward came to the door in his dressing gown. The giveaway was the trousers and shoes he was wearing beneath it. When he realised it was only me, he called everyone back in and after he had returned my torch, I went on my way.

The next day, I rode on to Galway Bay. There is a tradition in Ireland whereby musicians go to bars equipped with their instruments and play with whoever they meet. The tradition is kept alive more on the west coast and prevalent in Galway Bay. I spent the rest of my holiday there, but never told Peggy that I had only spent three nights in the cottage.

In 1984, I went on a mini tour of the North of Europe ending with a visit to my brother Dave, in Sittard, Southern Holland. When I was in Switzerland, I bought Dave a cuckoo clock. It was natural wood and deeply carved, which I thought would be more tasteful than the painted variety. Dave hung it on the wall, and it looked magnificent. The only problem was that every hour the cuckoo appeared and after a while, it became very irritating. When I came to leave, I was just five minutes up the road when I remembered I had left something behind, so I turned back. Dave must have heard me coming, for when I entered the house, I found him standing on a chair beneath the clock. He had a carving knife in his hand, pretending to be waiting for the cuckoo.

It was during this holiday, that I asked Dave to be the best man at my first wedding. He agreed, but he died before the wedding ever happened.

On a lighter note, Sue and I went to Malta for two weeks with Trevor and Kathie. It was a nice enough island, but two weeks was more than we needed. After a few days it became obvious that Kathie was content to sunbathe by the pool all day, so Sue and I hired a motorbike to explore the island. We both liked the old town of Valetta, and St Paul's Bay was beautiful. While in St Pauls Bay, it got late so we decided to eat there. We found a restaurant, which was half outside and partly on stilts over the bay. I ordered lobster, which is my favourite shellfish, but combined with the sea air, it was fabulous.

When Sue and I went on our boating holiday with Keith and Barbara, we picked up our cruiser from Reading and we headed towards the source of the Thames. The fact that none of us was experienced at piloting a boat, became apparent fairly quickly. When I was steering, I managed to collect half a tree. In truth, it was only a branch, but it looked like half a tree. When Keith was in charge, he nearly let the boat drift backwards into a weir!

I was looking for a replacement top hat for Chris Arden, so every time we moored, I searched every charity shop I could find, and I left a card. I had no luck during the holiday, but I did receive a phone call and subsequently, I bought a top hat.

We got as far as Oxford before we had to turn back. On our last night, Keith and I donned our dinner suits and the ladies wore their evening gowns. Keith and Barbara had even bought a floor standing candelabra. We then sang the songs of Gilbert and Sullivan, much to the amusement of the passers-by. It was a very civilised evening. The next day we returned the boat, which was unscathed, despite our best endeavours.

We also spent two weeks by Lago Maggiore in Northern Italy. We stayed in a hotel in Baveno, which was also friendly. It had been owned and run by the same family for generations and was allegedly where Churchill spent his honeymoon. We had paid for half board which is sometimes a risky business. The restaurant, however, was superb and we both enjoyed everything we tried.

On the first night, I liked the look of every desert, but I thought I would try profiteroles. They were very good, much larger than most, and filled with vanilla or chocolate cream. They were also covered with chocolate. They were so nice, in fact, that I chose them every other night. I soon became famous for always choosing them. One evening, instead of the waiter giving me my usual serving of three profiteroles, he presented me with the serving dish containing a huge pyramid of, maybe, a hundred profiteroles. I didn't show any reaction at all, but politely asked, 'do you have any cream?'

Lago Maggiore is so named because it is, by far, the largest of all the Italian lakes. It contains three islands. Isolabella, or the 'beautiful island', is famous for its palace and gardens, Isolpescatore, or 'Fisherman's Island', is famous for its fish restaurants. The last island is Isolmadre, or the 'mother island', the biggest of the three. Sue and I used the waterbus to frequent the islands and sometimes we had lunch on Isolapescatore.

On the far side of the lake was Switzerland, and the local bars and restaurants were happy to accept Italian lira. It was before the Euro was introduced. We took the waterbus to Switzerland and had lunch there. We discovered three types of Labatt larger. The nearest to the one found in Britain, was called Labatt Blue, they also had Labatt Red and Gold. They were all lovely!

In the late 1980's, Robert Heddon, bought a villa in Ibiza. Sue and I were among the first to be invited to go out there. The villa was built on a mountain, serviced by half a mile of private road. It consisted of three double bedrooms, two bathrooms, one, en suite to the master bedroom, and an enormous lounge. It also featured a swimming pool, an outside bar, and a pool table. Liz and I went there several times and on one occasion we decided to visit Formentera.

This was an adjacent, but much smaller island. The sea was as smooth as glass and we weren't taking the jeep, so we booked tickets for the small boat. However, on the return journey a storm blew up and the sea was very rough indeed. At one stage we were being chased by a twenty foot wave. I honestly thought it was our last day on earth. Even the crew looked worried, which was a sign of the danger we were in. We managed to outrun the wave before it broke, and we arrived safely in Ibiza. I have never been so happy to set foot on dry land.

I couldn't understand why people bought holiday homes, until Robert bought his villa. After a few visits it became a home from home. There is nowhere else that I have been, where I can relax within five minutes of arriving. During one visit, I noticed that Robert had bought two oil paintings. One of them was a beautiful typically Spanish shawl arranged over an antique chair. I took the painting outside and leant it against the villa, near the pool, and I photographed it. It wasn't until a few days later I discovered that it was painted by one of the prominent artists of the island and was worth a lot of money. I had the picture enlarged to its original size, and had it hand printed. It was so detailed that even the brush marks showed. Shortly afterwards, Sue and I invited Robert to dinner. He glanced at the photo and then gave it a double take because it was so realistic. Even the colours were like the real one. The only giveaway was the glass and the frame.

Over the years, my jobs at the villa ranged from being as simple as changing light bulbs, or descaling shower heads, to having a new marble kitchen worktop made to measure, to accommodate a new gas hob.

I have been to the villa about 15 times and over the years have visited with Sue, my mother, sister, younger brother, Kim, Mark, Pat and Liz. Liz and I even spent our honeymoon there. I remember us sitting on the terrace one fine evening drinking a bottle of Dom Perignon, which was bought as a wedding present by Liz's kids.

When Mum came with me to Ibiza, I gave her a guided tour of the island. One day, we were walking along a promenade, when Mum spotted Scott Michaelson sunbathing on the beach. He was, at the time, one of the stars of 'Neighbours, which was one of Mums' favourite soaps. She rather cheekily, asked him if her son could take a photo of her sitting next to him. He kindly agreed, so I got the photo.

I had it enlarged and framed and gave it to Mum to hang on her wall at home. She was very proud of it and showed it to everyone.

The time Mark joined me at the villa, I could hear swishing and cursing coming from his room on the first night. The next day, he explained that a mosquito had bitten him and drawn blood, and he was trying to swat it. Seeing the blood stain on the wall, I guessed he was successful.

Robert made a lot of improvements to the place. He had the private road tarmacked, turning it from a muddy track into a proper road. He had the electric sliding gates re-enabled so that they opened and shut by remote control. He replaced the awning over the pool table and the pool table itself, because the original had suffered water damage. He also replaced the furniture in both the dining room and the lounge. Finally, he replaced the satellite system to offer more English TV channels. His greatest success was, finding a Spanish housing manager who was willing to look after the villa. He was responsible for letting the villa, cleaning between guests and having all general maintenance carried out. This made me nearly, but not entirely, redundant, so Robert and I re-negotiated the terms of our agreement. I could no longer stay in the villa for free, but I did receive a generous discount.

One time, Sue and I arrived at the villa very early, before the cleaners had been. The previous guests had broken a window and left the shattered glass all over the patio. I didn't think it part of the cleaner's job, so I cleared it up. The following day,

I had it re glazed. It was simple enough for me to do, but very difficult for Robert to organize from England.

Over the years I have made a lot of friends, both Spanish and English expats. One day, I invited a few of the expats to 'my place' for a swim, a few drinks and nibbles. Pretentious perhaps, but it was how I was beginning to feel about the villa. Robert encouraged this view, because he knew I would look after the villa like it was my own.

In the late 1990's, Kim and I, went on a, 'two- resort', holiday to Venice and Lake Como. We chose an upmarket tour operator, and I was wondering if they were worth the extra money, until we started the holiday. The company insisted on exclusivity from every hotel they used and the accommodation in Venice was superb.

We did all the tourist things, including a trip in a Gondola and a visit to St Mark's Square. We then enjoyed a first class, train journey to Lake Como; our hotel there was fabulous and right next to the lake. On our last day, we were supposed to fly home in the morning, but when the rep arrived, she said that the flight had been delayed so we might as well enjoy another day in the sun. She then said the company would pay for all food and limited drinks. When we finally arrived at the airport, I felt sorry for the passengers who were on our flight but had come with a different tour company. They looked weary and fed up. The tour company opened another desk for us, checked in our bags, and led us to security and passport control. Were they worth the extra? Yes, they were.

On one of our holidays, Mark and I went down to the South of France. The route we chose, took us through the mountains of Eastern France. At one stage the view was spectacular, so

I wanted to take a photo. Mark, however, was driving like a thing possessed. I issued a few obscenities and expletives in response, and he, reluctantly, stopped. I took my photo, and then we sped on.

We stopped for the night in Lyon, and found a superb restaurant. We ordered a fruit de mare. It was on the menu as a starter for two people, so we weren't sure how it would be served. It came as a gigantic mountain of ice, embedded with clams, mussels, prawns, rings of squid and king prawns. For the main course we both chose steak. Now, I like my steak rare, but most French chef's cook steak extremely rare. In fact, if you cut the steak in half, the middle is almost raw. If you ordered 'bien cuit', or well done, you got a steak that was cooked, just well enough to ensure that even a good vet couldn't get it back on its feet. We both ordered 'bien cuit', so that what we received resembled a rare cooked, English steak. I was saving a piece of steak until last. As I came towards the end of my meal, a fork came from out of nowhere, and Mark ate my last piece of steak. I wouldn't have minded, but it was the best bit!

On our way home, we stopped for the night at Chateau Neuf du Pape. The next morning, we noticed that one of the smaller wine houses was open for tours. We decided to go on one, but when it came to the tasting, there appeared to be nowhere to spit the wine. We emerged, having drunk a lot of wine, at about 11a.m. . Neither of us felt like driving, so we had a sleep on the grass by the river. At about 1p.m. we bought some cheese, cold meats and bread and we had lunch by the river. After that, we felt a lot better, so we drove on.

Sue, and I, were crossing the English Channel by ferry. The sea was very rough, and we were surrounded by passengers looking decidedly unwell. Suddenly, there was an announcement over the 'tannoy' system, inviting people to upgrade to first class. We did so, for a change of environment, but there were two bonuses.

The stabilisers for the 'first class' dining room, were so good, that you could hardly feel the waves. Also, all food and drinks were included. One couple, sitting near us, were enjoying their food, and the man was drinking a lot of wine. He also had his car keys on the table, boasting an Aston Martin key fob. When we arrived in France, we made our way to the car deck, only to find a new Aston Martin DB9 and we wondered how he was going to drive it? At the last minute, he threw the keys to his wife. She sat behind the wheel, whilst he poured himself into the passenger seat.

During one holiday, Liz and I went to a Belgian theme bar called, 'Le Cochon Fidele', which translates to 'The Faithful Pig'. It offered about fifty Belgian beers, most of which had their own special glass. We ordered a cold plate for two. A big serving plate arrived, containing several cold meats and cheeses. When the waiter put it down in front of me, I realised it was for me and not a serving plate. Liz was brought the same, and we were given half a loaf of bread each. What we thought would be a light lunch turned out to be a feast.

In 2002 Liz and I, drove her daughter to Middlesbrough in time for her to enrol at the University of Teesside. It was a dismal day, made worse by the sight of urchins playing football in the street with a tin can, and in their bare feet. We checked into a hotel for the night, and we invited Tracy to join us for dinner. It was only 6 p.m. and the restaurant was empty, so we were surprised when they refused us a table. When I pointed out that we were guests, they reluctantly, agreed to serve us as long as we were gone by 7 p.m., because they were expecting a large coach party.

The tables were already laid, and they were foolish enough to light the candles. Suddenly a draft blew a paper menu onto the candle and set light to the table. I shouted 'Fire!'

But no one came. Finally, a waitress came and, nonchalantly, removed the burning remains, glaring at us as if we had started it. The food was mediocre, and the service was surly and slow. We will never stay there again.

After we had chosen Kefalonica, as our next destination, we discovered that one company offered a one bedroomed villa with its own swimming pool. This was quite a rarity, so we booked it immediately. There were only four villas surrounded by olive and lemon trees. I needed a lemon for my gin and tonic, so I took one from the ground. When we met the owner, I told him what I had done and he said, 'next time you want a lemon, please don't take mine from the ground.'

I thought he was angry until he added, 'always pick a fresh one from the tree.'

The package included a car, which we used to see the island. One day we drove to Lixouri and found a yacht for hire. The skipper offered to take three couples on a sailing trip, for the day, stopping for a cold lunch on board. We agreed to crew and, as the other two lads were younger and fitter than me, they dealt with the sails whilst, I took the wheel. Everything was fine, until I started talking. Whenever I turned around the yacht listed to port, or starboard. When we finally arrived back in Angostolli, we found a small restaurant to eat in. It reminded me of Corfu. They didn't speak any English, and they had no menu. Unfortunately, this time they also didn't understand Italian, so we just had to point, the food however was excellent. Overall, the holiday was superb, and I would recommend Kefalonia to anyone.

In 2009 we joined a very large holiday club, as trial members. This entitled us to 7 weeks holiday anywhere in the world. The first week however, had to be taken at Fuengirola, Costa del Sol. This was the location of their headquarters. The accommodation was the best either of us had ever stayed in. The lounge was large, and the en-suite bathroom contained a Jacuzzi bath that was big enough for a family of six! Also, on our patio was a Jacuzzi hot tub. We only went on one excursion, which was to Gibraltar. The excursion included a trip to see the Barbary apes. It is a nice place, but I wouldn't want to stay there for more than a few days.

Back at Fuengirola, there was a compulsory presentation, at which the company's best salesmen were very persuasive in extolling the virtues of full membership. They even showed us a promotional film starring Jenny Bond, who was saying how good the company and all its products were. We decided that the maintenance was too high, and although they had accommodation in most parts of the world, they didn't have any where we planned to go.

The next holiday we took with them was Tenerife. The accommodation couldn't have been more of a contrast. The sleeping arrangements were more fitting for a younger person, whose back might be more resilient. We complained, but they couldn't find us another room for two days, so we found another hotel. The company finally upgraded us to a very acceptable room.

We went up Mt. Teide, which is a dormant volcano. A cable car took us halfway up and we walked the rest.

We spent a fabulous week in Scotland, in a lovely hotel near Stirling, but next to the famous golf course of Gleneagles. We took the train to Edinburgh and then hired a car for the rest of the journey. We wanted a restful holiday, so we didn't drive very far. We did reach Pitlochry, where we did a walking tour. It was a pretty town and well worth the visit. Although Scotland is famous for its rain, the weather was kind to us. We saw beautiful scenery and snow-capped mountains. The people were very friendly and one lady, in Perth, gave us directions to the cathedral. She also gave us her phone number and asked us to visit her. We found the cathedral very friendly and were even mentioned in dispatches. On our last day we met our newfound friend, for a coffee, and she gave us some mementoes of our visit.

There was nothing spectacular about this holiday, but we had had a great time and vowed to return.

The following year, we went to Goa, which was my favourite destination. We stayed in a splendid hotel, with a large pool and a spa pool, which we virtually had to ourselves.

On the first day, we hailed a taxi to take us to the nearest town to change some money. The driver showed us to a place of exchange, which turned out to offer the best rate of the holiday. It was street market day, so we spent some time looking at the stalls before we returned to the hotel. On the way back, our driver Sanjay, offered to chauffer us the next day for only £14. It was too good an offer to refuse, so we arranged to meet him the next day. He was, such a lovely man we went with him every other day. He took us to several places, many of which were devoid of any other tourists. We saw several Hindu temples and a large impressive waterfall. We climbed on an elephants' back to wash it, or rather it washed us. It loaded up its trunk with water and sprayed it all over us. We also rode on an elephant, which Liz had done before, but I had never so much as touched one.

One day, we asked Sanjay to take us to a nice but non-touristy restaurant. He chose one of his favourites, so we invited him to join us as our guest. It was as well we did because the menu was in Hindu with no English translation. Sanjay ordered for us and the food was excellent.

Near our hotel, there were restaurants in both directions. One was run by French man, and although it was expensive, it offered a very romantic setting and the food was fabulous. Nearby, we both enjoyed a full body massage, which we found very relaxing.

One bird of prey, which is very rare in the UK but commonplace in Goa, is the Brahminy Kite. I spotted one flying so high that I could only just see it. With the 48 times zoom lens of my camera, I was able to take a photo of it. Back at home, I downloaded it onto the computer and enlarged it further. I was surprised to see that it was looking at me, no doubt smiling for the camera!

For our last holiday, we chose The Algarve, Portugal, for two weeks, and we hired a car from a company next to the airport. We used the car to drive to and from the resort and to explore the Algarve. We drove to Sea life. This was included in the excursions, but it felt much 'freer' to go on our own. We saw the dolphins, sea lions and the killer whale performing. We also

189

saw the birds of prey flying outside and a show of the more colourful exotic birds inside. The choice of lunch was somewhat limited, but no more than you would expect in such a place.

Despite having a car, we joined two of the excursions. One was to see Cliff Richards's vineyard, and to sample his wine. The other one was to Lisbon, which was good to see. We took a tram to the base of the castle, which towered over the city. We then walked by the river and had a delicious lunch by the square.

Back at the resort, we tried their restaurant. We found the food bland, none of the choices on the menu were remotely Portuguese. Stepping out of the resort again was a liberating experience. There were so many restaurants, we were spoilt for choice. They were varied in price and quality, but we never found a bad one.

Although the resorts varied greatly, in both design and layout, they all had one thing in common. You could be anywhere in the world and not know where, until you left the resort.

We were glad we joined the club as temporary members, because, we went to places we might not have gone to, otherwise. However, there were two things that irritated both of us. One was the 'organised fun' element, and the other, was the hordes of salesmen who were continually trying to persuade you to upgrade. At one resort, we met an elderly couple who had been members for decades. They were diamond members, which was one of the highest memberships. Despite this, they were continually badgered to upgrade.

I would like to end this chapter with a story of a conversation which Oscar Wilde, allegedly, had with an American tourist. The American lady was on holiday in England for the first time and was listening to some Mozart music at a concert in London. Oscar Wilde was at the same concert. After the concert finished and he learnt that the American was in England for the first time, he was keen to engage her in conversation. He asked if she had enjoyed the concert, to which she replied that she had very much, and she asked him, 'is Mozart still composing?'

Oscar gave a wry smile and said, 'No Madam, I think you will find that he is decomposing.'

Chapter 21

Back to the future

We have travelled full circle and arrive back in the present day. I am now enjoying my life at home with Liz. My body is still paralyzed, but now I have a wonderful team of carers who help me with all my needs.

I still have a lot of visitors and I am able to get out and about, as we have an adapted vehicle. When the weather is good, we can go across the road to our local park, or we can visit some of the National Trust sites that are not too far away. Liz has also discovered the Westerham Brewery, which is wheelchair accessible, and has a tap room, and tasters of different beers, Liz has to bring a teaspoon for me, so I can have a taste, she won't let me have more than a teaspoon though!

By this point, some of you may have concluded that I must have nine lives, like a cat. If I have, I figure I have used eight of them. So, I'd better be more careful in future. Apparently, there are fewer than 400 people in the UK with 'Locked-In Syndrome'; with those odds I could have won the Lottery.

I was at The Raphael for over six years, which was a bit of a shock, especially as I had only been admitted to hospital twice before in my life. Once at the age of three, and again at the age of six, when I had my tonsils removed. I don't remember the operation, the only thing I remember is the ice cream afterwards.

Paralysis presents many problems, not the least of which is, that if I develop an itch, I am unable to scratch it. Similarly, if a wasp lands on the end of my nose, all I can do is watch it and hope it doesn't sting me. In truth, I never have been stung, probably because I don't,or rather can't, do anything to provoke it, but the fear is always there. I would be deluding myself if I claimed not to miss some of my past life. In fact, I miss all of it, but there are three things I miss above all else: **holding my wife; eating and drinking normally; and singing.**

Veronika, one of the Neuro psychology assistants here, wasn't at all surprised when I said I thought my long-term memory and my creative ability had both improved.

'After all,' she said, 'most of your senses are either missing, or have been severely impaired. It follows, therefore, that your remaining senses have been enhanced.'

The years since my stroke have taught me two things. Firstly, I should always focus on what I can do, not on what I can't do. Secondly, I should never lose faith that one day I will make a full recovery. A good example of the first is that, if I had not had the stroke I probably wouldn't have started writing, and I certainly wouldn't have written this particular book. I have also written three short stories and learnt a few words in 26 different languages. Although my body is paralyzed, I try to keep my mind active.I have planned many things for Liz and I to do together, including holidays and going to the opera. Unfortunately, I can't realise any of these plans until I have recovered.

My body doesn't move, so cannot generate heat. Even when I am told the room is warm, I am still cold. Raymond, my occupational therapist, has designed a communication system for me. It is similar to existing systems, but it divides the alphabet into three sets. I blink to indicate the set and again to indicate the letter within the set. The system works well if I only want to say a few words, but if I want to say more, it is very long winded. Lately, I have regained a lot of movement in my mouth and Liz has learnt to partly lip read. This makes the whole process quicker. All the staff at The Raphael Hospital, have treated me extremely well, but I was there a long time. As my grandad used to say, 'I'll be glad when I have had enough of this!'

Now I am home, I can feel like more than just a visitor in my own home and can start to live again and try to recover. It is only while writing this book that I realise how much I have crammed into my life. However, there are many places to go to, people to see and things to do. I withdraw nothing from my previous statement. I am glad I had the stroke. It has given me time to reflect on what sort of person I used to be. My conclusion is that I was not a bad person, but there is plenty of room for improvement. I have many failings but the greatest of them all is my lack of patience, tolerance and forgiveness. The things which have helped me most to endure this darkest hour are my faith, my wife, the staff of Tobias House, my many visitors and my sense of humour.

Medical Science does move on, sometimes very quickly, I will NOT give up on my recovery. I have made improvements in some areas, my face is much more expressive, more people are able to lip read, and I am able to breathe a bit more on my own, also, my muscles are improving.

I would like to say one final word to my fellow 'Locked-In Syndrome' sufferers. There is light at the end of the tunnel. It may be an extremely long tunnel with a very small light at the end of it, but you will get there.

THE END

The Friends

She reaches up to the sky and feels the warmth of the sun. She feels close to nature. She never wants to return to the town where she lives.

He has walked along this towpath many times before, but this time he will return alone. His father has said that if the horse can't carry a load he must go, so the boy is taking the horse to an animal sanctuary.

He is returning to home with his shoulder sloped. It is his favourite place in the world, but he is inconsolable. The horse was his only friend and he has had to say goodbye. Just then he sees a young girl coming towards him. He senses her sadness.

As their paths cross, he dares to speak to her, and they are instantly drawn to each other. They are both on their way home, but neither is in any hurry. They sit on the grass bank and talk for hours.

They exchange names, she is Kim, and his name is Sam. She explains that this morning she felt close to nature and never wanted to go home. He told her how he had to say goodbye to his horse. After speaking for some time, they realise it is so late that they have to go home.

They meet the next day and every day for weeks and months. Then, one day her father tells her that they are moving away. The next day they meet at their special place and she breaks the news to him. She says that they should say goodbye now rather than later. His eyes are full of tears as he slopes home.

She hates to see him like this, but she is sure that if they leave it to the last minute the pain will be worse. Several days later she is hanging around the house when her father comes home and says that he has decided not to move away. He knows how much the place means to her and it would be unfair to move away. Besides, he can keep his job with the firm; he just has to give up his promotion.

His family's happiness comes first. Kim is so overjoyed, she flings her arms around her father's neck, kissing and hugging him.

Then she runs to her favourite spot by the river, hoping to find Sam, but he is not there. She returns there every day and waits all day. Then one day Sam comes shuffling down the towpath, looking very sad indeed. When she sees Sam, she runs to him with outstretched open arms and embraces him.

Then she takes his hand and leads him to their favourite place. When she tells him her good news, his eyes fill with tears again but this time they are tears of joy. They both know that this has become much more than just a friendship. They can be together forever.

The End.

The Village

Tom was standing in his bedroom looking worried. A crumpled letter lay at his feet. He gazed through the window at his beautiful back garden and the glorious golden field of wheat beyond. Tom had lived in his cottage all his life. He was born there and two years ago, when his parents had died, he had inherited the cottage.

His cottage was situated in the idyllic Kent village town of Appledore. All the cottages were built of stone and like his, most were adorned with thatched rooves. The village church was also built of stone and was over six hundred years old. The village had two pubs, both of which served real ale. One was Tom's favourite because it sold a big selection of beer and served good food.

The crumpled letter on the floor was one of many sent by the government to all the villagers. It announced the construction of a motorway on the outskirts of the village. It was to pass through the farmer's field, only fifty feet from the end of his garden. Once it was built the noise from the traffic would decimate the peace and quiet that had been enjoyed by the village for centuries.

Tom was relatively lucky, the motorway would not pass near enough to his property to justify a compulsory purchase. Others in the village were not so fortunate. Their cottages would be compulsorily purchased and subsequently, demolished.

Tom was sure that a petition would be raised, but even if all the villagers were to sign it there would be fewer than a thousand signatures which wouldn't be enough to influence a government.

They reinforced the petition with meetings and marches in the village, and they invited both the local and the national press to cover the story. They organised a peaceful demonstration outside the Houses of Parliament and they even invited the TV people. However, the government would not be moved, and they confirmed that the motorway would be built as planned. The villagers were furious, and they took the matter to court. They thought that they had a strong case, but they lost. The villagers were about to give up hope when they heard that their two nearest towns would also be affected by the impending motorway and they raised their own petitions. One town was just under nine miles west of the village and the other town eight miles east.

When everyone had signed, one petition contained almost twenty-five thousand signatures and the other petition contained over ten thousand. This was enough to sway the government and it was announced that the motorway would be re-routed to avoid both towns and the village. The villages and townsfolk were overjoyed but that joy was short-lived. At this stage, the contractor got involved. The government were told that the dispute had already caused a delay but now the motorway was to be re-routed the delay would be considerable. In terms of time and materials the contractor's best estimate was that it would cost nearly £1,000,000. When the government was appraised of the cost of the detour, they took it very seriously and decided to reinstate the original route of the motorway.

This came as very bad news for the townsfolk and the

villagers, so they decided to club together and bring the case before the Appeal Court. This was at the Royal Courts of Justice in The Strand, London. On the appointed day hundreds of people went to the court. Twelve people were chosen to represent the others during the case and of the rest, only one hundred could be admitted owing to the limited size of the public gallery. They appointed the best barrister they could afford, and they were confident that this time they had a very strong case. They could show that there were two towns also affected by the motorway and thousands of additional homes.

Hordes of government officials came, and of course they had their own counsel. They also brought along the senior manager to represent the contractor. The rest of the townsfolk and the villagers remained outside, patiently waiting for their friends to return. The case was over sooner than expected and the first of their friends emerged triumphant. They announced that they had won the case and the motorway would be re-routed. They also said that the government had been ordered to pay all of their costs.

Back in the towns and the village, there was cause for much celebration and rejoicing. The Mayor of the village held a meeting in the biggest venue he could find, which was the theatre. For the benefit of those that were not at court, he announced the result of the case. The ensuing parties and fireworks continued for a week and the two pubs did a roaring trade.

Tom gazed out of his bedroom window looking at his beautiful garden and the golden wheat field beyond, and for the first time since the letter from the government arrived, he was able to smile.

The Masks

Jimmy had enjoyed dressing up for as long as he could remember, but now he was collecting grotesque masks to scare people with. He would lurk in the shadows and jump out on poor unsuspecting passers-by. One day he even gave an old lady a heart attack, but he didn't care, he was just having fun.

He continued for months, every time finding a new hiding place. He knew the police were after him, but it just added to the excitement. One night when he returned home, he removed his costume as usual but when he tried to take off the mask it wouldn't move. He struggled and struggled, but no matter how hard he tried the mask would not budge. He started to panic; what if the mask never came off?

Beads of sweat started to run from his forehead and tears started to flow from his eyes. He had never before believed in anyone but himself, but he fell to his knees and prayed. He prayed for half an hour, but nothing happened. Then he realised if he didn't know who he was praying to, he couldn't expect answers. He prayed to God and promised that he would never again scare anyone. Suddenly the mask came off and he cried tears of joy and relief. Then he remembered his promise which was one promise he would have to keep.

He collected his masks and headed for the incinerator at the end of the garden. On his return he felt sad because he had lost his masks, but he also felt strangely elated, as if a huge weight had been lifted from his shoulders. He felt better than he had ever felt in his life.

Jimmy spent the next few weeks tracking down the people to whom he had caused the most distress. He found most of their addresses by following them home. When he found the old lady, whom he had caused to have a heart attack, he sent her a lovely big bouquet of flowers.

On the accompanying card he wrote just one word which expressed his remorse, it read 'Sorry'. He seemed to find much more satisfaction from being nice to people than he ever had from scaring people. It was a new experience; he had never been nice to anybody and nobody had ever been nice to him.

When he had destroyed the masks, he had kept one back. He was determined to scare people one more time to find out what he really felt. He put on his costume, as usual, and then donned his one remaining mask.

Jimmy hid in the shadows waiting to pounce, but he had made one big mistake; he had returned to his favourite location and the police were lying in wait. They had been waiting for two weeks, each day changing their location, but always returning to the same place, which was Jimmy's favourite spot. This time they were lucky; Jimmy was not... they caught him and fired a Taser gun at him. Their excuse for using a Taser was that they thought he had a gun.

Jimmy didn't own a gun; he wouldn't know what to do with one if he had one. He felt his body writhe and shake from the effect of a forty thousand volt shock. The convulsions continued long after the shock had subsided and sadly, he didn't recover.

Jimmy would never again scare anyone.

Jimmy would never again do anything.

ACKNOWLEDGEMENTS

I would like to thank my wife Liz for undertaking the arduous task of translating my blinks into words. I would also like to thank Esther and Lisa for typing the book and to Dr. Anita, and Veronika for acting as my editor. Also, to Daniel and Hayley for drawing my caricature on the front cover of this book. My thanks too to my publisher James Essinger, to Charlotte Mouncey for her work on the cover and for the typesetting, to Fran Garratt for her assistance with editing and to Margaret Dowley MBE for her help with formatting the book.

I would also like to thank the carers who have looked after me in hospital and at home. These include Lovely, Eva, Violina, Florentina, Costel, Sister Mary, Georgiana, Cedric, Mihaela, Natalie, Sarah, Sharon, Joel, David, Rosalinda and Luminita.

The book is dedicated to Liz, Esther, Lisa, Professor Barbara, Dr. Anita, Veronika, Daniel and Hayley. To my cousin Bobbi, who died in 2013, to my friends Robert Hedden and Vivienne Taylor and my wife's ex-husband Malcolm Bragg who died in 2015. It is also dedicated to all my many visitors, especially those who have suffered me almost once a week. Finally, it is dedicated to my fellow sufferers of Locked-In Syndrome, and to three friends who passed away after I had finished the book Diana, Marion and Betty.